Can We Talk?

A Financial Guide for Baby Boomers Assisting Their Elderly Parents

BOB MAUTERSTOCK

Soar
with
Eagles

A Publisher Driven
by Vision and Purpose
www.soarhigher.com

Can We Talk?
A Financial Guide for Baby Boomers Assisting Their Elderly Parents

Copyright © 2008 by Robert B. Mauterstock, Jr., CFP, All rights reserved.

ISBN-10: 0-9771403-9-3
ISBN-13: 978-0-9771403-9-8
Library of Congress Control Number 2008938109

First Edition

Published by

1200 North Mallard Lane
Rogers, AR 72756, USA
www.soarhigher.com

Editing by Lauren Helper
Content development assistance by Annie Douglass
Cover, interior design, and editing by Carrie Perrien Smith
Photography by Shane Kato

Printed in the United States of America

Contents

Lifefolio

Dedication

**This book is dedicated to
my mother and father, Ruth and Bob Mauterstock,
who inspired me to live a life that makes a difference.**

Acknowledgements

My sincere thanks go to all of the families I have worked with over the years who have given me the background that confirmed the importance of this book.

To my wonderful wife, Mary, who has always inspired me to stretch myself.

To my beautiful daughter, Stephanie, who has supported me in whatever activity I undertake.

To my team at KR Wealth Management who helped me make a difference in the lives of our clients and especially to Kevin Leahy who has been my partner for eight years.

To the friends that I value very dearly who took the time to read my drafts and give me valuable feedback, Jeanne Connell, Andy Miser, and Margaret Greenberg.

To Lauren Helper of Hidden Helpers who edited my book and encouraged me, chapter by chapter, to get it done.

To Annie Douglass of Sticky Rice Solutions who organized and designed the forms I created for the Lifefolio.

To Carrie Perrien Smith of Soar With Eagles who brought the whole project together, designed the book covers and format, did final editing, and got it published.

To Dave Pugh of John Wiley and Sons who taught me what the commercial publishing world was really like.

To Jerry D. Simmons of writersreaders.com who gave me valuable advice in the direction I should take to get my book published.

Chapter 1
Financial Challenges Facing Baby Boomers and Their Parents

I have been a financial advisor to hundreds of families over the last 30 years. All in all, it has been a very satisfying career, but time and time again, I have observed heartbreaking financial situations that could have been avoided.

Most of the parents of Baby Boomers (like me) went through the Great Depression. They understood what it meant not to have any money. As a result, they never wasted money. They bought modest homes and lived frugal lives. My mother would never throw anything away that could be fixed; my parents didn't even have a credit card. The parents of our generation saved their money and saw their modest homes increase in value to 10 to 20 times more than what they had originally paid for them.

And now our parents are reaching the end of their lives. They are passing on their decades-long savings to their children. When they die, the value of their homes is stepped up to current value and their children inherit that tremendous gain, totally income tax free. We are in the midst of the largest transfer of wealth in the history of man. It is projected that over the next 20 years, $25 trillion will pass to the Baby Boomers from their parents!

It is projected that over the next 20 years, $25 trillion will pass to the Baby Boomers from their parents!

This is a tremendous financial opportunity for Baby Boomer children, if handled correctly. Unfortunately, many Baby Boomers experience pitfalls that diminish that wealth and cause great turmoil within a family. These problems often develop while the parents are alive and can be corrected when the Boomers and their parents work together to do some financial planning. But too often, the cost of long-term care, lack of communication between family members, and poor estate planning can turn a financial blessing into a financial nightmare. I have seen it happen too many times. Let me give you an example.

One of my clients is a retired orthopedic surgeon. Twenty years ago, his mother passed away. Without discussing it with her children, she decided she would leave her savings and investment assets to one son and her waterfront home to the other. At the time, they were approximately equal in value. My client was lucky enough to inherit the home. Over the last 20 years, it has increased in value to more than a million dollars. But at the same time, the other son's inherited investments struggled through the meltdown of 2001–2002 and are hardly worth more than when he got them. As a result, he felt cheated by his mother. He only spoke to my client (his brother) through a lawyer. Last year, the brother who felt cheated passed away after a long illness without speaking to his only brother or seeing him for more than 10 years.

This type of situation happens all the time. Most elderly parents are not willing to discuss their financial position with their children. They were taught never to talk to anyone about how much money they had, especially their children. As a result, they aren't aware of, or don't adequately understand, the myriad of issues or problems that can jeopardize their financial assets, and their children have no idea how to help them.

Most Baby Boomer children are not willing to take the initiative and talk to their parents about money. Just asking their parents how much money they have or where their investments are can make the adult child extremely uncomfortable. Many parents might respond with, "Well, why do you want to know? Do you want my money?" Just asking the question often puts the adult child at risk, making him or her look greedy.

So, if parents are resistant or even unwilling to talk to their children about money and children are afraid that bringing up the subject will make them look greedy, where do we go from here? Continuing to avoid the topic is a formula for miscommunication, misunderstanding, and ultimate disaster.

In my 30 years as a financial advisor, I have helped many families make important financial decisions in planning their family's financial future. I have seen many intergenerational financial programs develop and become reality. I have observed what works and what doesn't. I have developed a series of steps that have proven to unlock the silence between Boomers and their parents to allow them to communicate freely and develop an intergenerational financial plan that works.

That's why I chose to write this book. I wanted to help families who are struggling to help each other preserve the family's assets, provide for all the parents' needs, and offer a meaningful legacy to their children and grandchildren.

Where do we start? First, we'll set the stage for a family meeting. But this meeting has to be planned carefully and include all the right players — outside professionals, the parents, and the children. If everybody doesn't do their homework ahead of time, this meeting will not accomplish anything and might even leave things in a worse state than before.

Once the family meeting occurs, real dialogue can develop and the parents and their children can begin to prepare for all the obstacles they face in preserving their wealth. One of these hurdles is the impact of long-term care on the family finances. If parents are no longer able to make financial decisions, legal issues of competency need to be addressed. The parents' investment portfolio needs to be structured to weather the storm and provide the income the parents need, as well as offer some growth for the next generation if that is desired. Taxes also need to be addressed. What structures are most efficient at minimizing estate and income taxes on both the state and federal level?

Fortunately, you will find the answers to these questions in the coming chapters. In addition, in the last chapter you will find a number of forms that can help you organize your parents' financial affairs and avoid the difficulties that I will discuss in the book.

The Bottom Line

If you follow the steps that I have outlined in this book, your relationship with your parents regarding money will dramatically change. You will feel a new freedom to discuss what is really important with them in a way that they don't feel threatened or taken advantage of. As a result, the remaining years that you have together with your parents will be more meaningful and have a positive impact on the family for years to come.

The Current Financial State of Baby Boomers and Their Parents

Chapter 2
Setting the Stage
For a Family Meeting

Transforming your relationship with your parents about money is not an easy task. With the right tools, though, you can do it. You will be able to discuss issues and topics that were previously off-limits and figure out ways to work in tandem with your parents to improve, modify, or change their financial circumstances. You will have a new sense of freedom in your communication with each other and no longer fear the forbidden topics of money and death.

To get to this place, you will have to take a series of well-planned steps that require your patience and persistence. The first step is to plan a *family meeting* to sit down with your parents, review their finances, and help them make plans for their future. This family meeting is an integral part of your new relationship and has a number of different pieces that need to be put in place before the meeting occurs. If these pieces are not prepared properly, the family meeting can become a disaster; resulting in hurt feelings, anger, and possibly the breakdown of all financial communication.

One of my clients is a successful business owner. He felt that he could set up a financial meeting with his parents just like he might do with the key people in his business. He decided that part of the traditional family gathering for Thanksgiving would be allocated to talking to Mom and Dad about their finances and giving them advice for their future plans. He announced at the Thanksgiving dinner table that the meeting would start shortly after dessert.

His parents felt that they should have been warned that such a meeting would occur. Their perception was that the children were ganging up on them and forcing them to do things that they didn't want to do. My client ran the meeting, which involved himself and his wife, his two sisters and their spouses, and of course, his parents. Early in the meeting it became clear that his parents didn't want to share their financial information with their children's spouses. My client realized this and asked all the spouses to leave. One of the sister's husbands felt that it was important for him to be there and a shouting match ensued. The whole meeting became about who should be there and who shouldn't and quickly deteriorated. Not only did my client not get the meeting he wanted, but his parents have since resisted any efforts to get the family together again to discuss their finances.

The family meeting should be planned well in advance to avoid any such nasty surprises. One of the most important things to do first is to identify who amongst the children is most appropriate to coordinate and lead the meeting. This is the child that parents can easily communicate with, the child that they are comfortable discussing their personal affairs with, and the child who has no fear in asking them important questions.

Who is the Alpha Child?

The Allianz Life Insurance Company conducted a study they called *The American Legacies Study*. I will refer to their research several times in this book. They gathered information by conducting over 2,000 interviews with Baby Boomers and their parents. One of the findings their study revealed was the existence of the *alpha child*. This is the child that keeps the family connected, who is always the first to make sure that family gatherings occur on a consistent basis, and communicates often with his siblings and parents. He or she is the child who the parents are most comfortable discussing money issues with. This is the person we want to organize and co-facilitate the family meeting.

One of the most important things to do first is to identify who amongst the children is most appropriate to coordinate and lead the meeting.

Since you have taken the time to pick up this book and realize the importance of this subject, the alpha child in your family may be you. Examine your relationship with your parents. If the above listed characteristics describe you, then it is most likely that you are that person. But don't let your ego get in the way. Be objective in your evaluation of your relationship with your parents and your siblings' relationship with them. If you are married, discuss it with your spouse and ask for his or her feedback.

Obviously if you are the only child, you may think that you don't have a choice. But in some cases if you are the only child, your spouse may act in the capacity as the alpha child. Your parents may have more confidence in talking over issues with him or her than they do with you. After all, you are their child and they may never give your opinions the same weight as your spouse or another person outside the family. Your husband/wife might be brilliant in your parents' eyes. There is no reason why you shouldn't take advantage of this situation. I am an only child and I have acted as my mom's financial advisor since my dad passed away almost 10 years ago. But every time I give her an investment recommendation and it works out, she seems to remember that it was an idea my wife came up with. So whenever we need to discuss an important financial issue with her, I discuss it with my wife first and she will often propose it to Mom. It has a much better chance of getting adopted than if I brought it up.

Working with Your Parents' Trusted Advisors

The second person you want to involve in the family meeting is one of your parents' trusted advisors. In your own case, your most trusted advisor might be your financial planner or your accountant. But that might not be true for your parents. In their generation, they might not have had much contact with a financial planner. They may never have used an accountant to prepare their taxes. Take a look at their situation. Who did they turn to when they had a family crisis? Who have they sought out when they had financial questions? That is the person you want. It may be a family lawyer, a local bank executive, or even a minister, rabbi, or priest. The important thing is that your parents are comfortable with the individual and trust his or her advice.

Now that you have identified the two key players in your family meeting, ask them to help you prepare for the event. If you have done a good job identifying them, then you should have no trouble getting them involved. The alpha child will organize the event itself. He or she will coordinate the date with your parents and your siblings. It is probably best not to tie it to a regular family gathering. It would be difficult to have grandchildren and spouses in the house when you are trying to have a serious discussion. There might be too many distractions. I suggest that if your parents are mobile, you should have the family meeting in the office of the trusted advisor. This will provide a neutral, business-like setting free of distractions. But if they are particularly anxious about travel — or about having the meeting at all — have the meeting in their home.

The trusted advisor's role will be to present the idea of the family meeting to your parents and convince them (if necessary) that it is a good idea and will benefit the family. He or she will also share with them a list of topics to be discussed at the meeting. *The Allianz American Legacies Study* is a great resource. The thousands of Boomers and parents that were surveyed concluded that there were four areas that most families considered important to discuss:

- Values and life lessons
- Instructions and wishes to be fulfilled
- Personal possessions of emotional value
- Family assets and real estate

Creating the Family Meeting Agenda

The first and probably most comfortable area for the parents to talk about is " Values and Life Lessons." These are beliefs that the parents consider important to be passed on from one generation to the next. They may include family customs and traditions the parents want continued, faith and religious-based beliefs, and memoirs and stories that should be shared. One of my clients is completing a written memoir to present to his family to preserve his family's history and their experience as Jews in Hungary during World War II. Another client wants to make sure that the entire family continues to get together every Thanksgiving as the family has done for three generations. He feels that this gathering is important to maintain the family continuity. Discussing values and life lessons provides the opportunity for parents to share those beliefs, stories, and customs that they want to see continued after they are gone.

The second area to be discussed is "Instructions and Wishes to be Fulfilled." Each parent has certain things that they want to make sure are taken care of when they are gone, and these wishes must be passed on to other family members. For example, one of my clients has a child who is mentally challenged and has not been able to live alone and take care of herself.

Discussing values and life lessons provides the opportunity for parents to share those beliefs, stories, and customs that they want to see continued after they are gone.

Her parents have taken care of her for her entire life. Once the parents are gone, they do not expect their other children to take her in, but they do want to make sure she is placed in a group home and lives a comfortable life. They have made provisions in their will for her financial care.

Sometimes parents want to make sure that a family member is able to get an education or a child is able to buy a home. These wishes need to be discussed. Finally, the parents' final wishes need to be made known. What type of funeral or memorial service do they want? Where do they want to be buried? Do they want to be cremated? This is often a very difficult topic for anyone to face, but it has been my experience that once it is addressed and plans are discussed, parents feel relieved and can move on to other things. But if these issues are not brought up, misunderstanding and hurt feelings can often result.

Just recently, one of my clients died. She was ninety-two, but had never made it clear to her children what type of memorial service she wanted and where she wanted to be buried. Her two children fought for over two months to determine where she should be buried. One said that she wanted to be buried next to her husband. The other stated that her mother's friend, Doris, had told her that she wanted to be buried with her parents in a location much farther away. The second child won, but now the children are not talking to each other.

The third topic to be discussed at the family meeting is "Personal Possessions of Emotional Value." Are there certain pieces of furniture, musical instruments, or jewelry that a parent wants to make sure are passed on to a favorite niece, nephew, or grandchild? My mother wants to make sure that a piece of furniture she inherited from her mother goes to one of her nephews. Some possessions have enormous emotional value to their owners. A favorite set of golf clubs, a photo album, or a special jade ring can often become a very special gift to a family member that reminds them of their aunt, uncle, parent, or grandparent for many years. Think of your own family. Are there certain valuables that you want to make sure get passed on to certain people?

The fourth and last topic to be discussed at the family meeting is the one probably most difficult to discuss, "Family Assets and Real Estate." I don't believe it is important at this meeting for parents to be specific as to who will get what, but I do think it is important that the family know what the resources are. This is a very valuable exercise for parents to conduct. It forces them to do an inventory of their assets, where they are, what account they might be in, and what they are worth. Often couples will have bank accounts and CDs at a number of different banks. Deposits for pensions and Social Security may go to different accounts. It can often be quite confusing for children to uncover.

Although it seems like a very difficult and perhaps impossible task, I assure you that once the family meeting occurs, everyone in the family will be thankful.

If there is any substantial family real estate, such as a shoreline or mountain vacation home, it is very important to discuss the future of this real estate. I have seen too many times that a valuable piece of real estate becomes a wedge that tears a family apart. One child may be passionate about keeping the property in the family, while another lives far away and just wants the cash. It can create enormous discord between family members.

The parents and children must sit down along with the trusted advisor and outline all the options available to them. Each child must make clear what their wishes are. Then the parents need to take some time with their advisor to discuss the impact of different choices. If the parents do not make a decision regarding the disposition of a valuable family property and it is left to the executor, I can assure you that it will become a very difficult family issue.

Preparing Yourself for the Family Meeting

Once the trusted advisor has discussed the agenda for the family meeting with the parents and the alpha child has coordinated everyone's schedule, you are ready to have the meeting. Although it seems like a very difficult and perhaps impossible task, I assure you that once the family meeting occurs, everyone in the family will be thankful. For many families, issues like finances and death have carefully been avoided at family gatherings for years. But it is on everyone's mind. It's like the big white elephant that sits in the middle of the room that everyone tries to avoid but cannot overlook. Once communication has opened up and the four areas I have recommended have been discussed, a burden has been lifted from the family. There is a lightness and freedom to discuss topics that were left unsaid for a long time. Future family gatherings will be less stressful because doubt has been removed and everyone knows where he or she stands. Your parents will experience much more comfort and less anxiety facing the problems of growing old knowing now that the family is working with them.

You may find that one or two family members will try to undermine the meeting, using the excuse that it will upset your parents or will uncover old issues that shouldn't be discussed. But don't let them deter you. Consider the alternative. Do you want to keep everyone in the dark until after your parents have passed away and then deal with everything in a crisis mode? Or do you want to discuss things rationally and clearly with your parents and siblings so that everyone is included? The choice is yours. But if one of your siblings does not want to participate or warns you that an open conversation with your parents is dangerous, thank them for expressing their opinion, but do not be deterred from having the meeting. Encourage them to attend. Consider recording the meeting (either audio or video) and providing them with a copy. Get them involved any way you can. You do not want them coming back to you five years after your parents have died and inferring that everything was done your way and they didn't have any say. Don't give them that weapon to use against you.

The Bottom Line

If you can identify the alpha child in your family, work with your parents' trusted advisor, and put together a meaningful agenda, you can conduct a very successful family meeting. This family meeting will alter your relationship with your parents and set the stage for successful future dealings with them.

Chapter 3
The Family Meeting: A Case Study

The following is an example of what you might be able to expect at a family meeting based on real-life reports. Your family meeting will undoubtedly differ from this one. But I hope this gives you an idea of what can go right and can go wrong at your own family meeting.

The Smiths' Family Meeting (as Told by Jim Smith)

Finally the day had arrived and we were about to have the much-anticipated family meeting. I picked up my sister, Carolyn, at the airport, and my brother, John, drove down from Boston. It was a struggle getting them both here. John kept reminding me that his two sons are involved in soccer and they couldn't miss any games. I assured him that he would only be gone for a day and his wife, Marge, could get them to the games. Carolyn complained that she'd had to cancel a weekend strategy session with two of her peers at work, but I assured her that this meeting would be well worth her sacrifice.

With my parents' consent, we had agreed to hold the meeting at our parents' home on Emerson Road, since Mom was having a great deal of difficulty getting around due to the arthritis in both her knees. Both Mom and Dad suggested that their longtime friend and banker, Bunker Raymond, act as the trusted advisor and facilitator of the meeting. Mr. Raymond had been president of one of the local banks for many years, and he helped Dad get his insurance business started many years ago. Even though he had been retired for a while, Mr. Raymond was still very sharp and had a great sense of humor.

When I approached Mr. Raymond about facilitating the meeting, I visited him at his spacious old colonial home on Sunset Ridge. I explained to him what a family meeting was, the four areas we wanted to discuss, and how important the process was to the whole family. At first, I wasn't sure how he would respond. He had a puzzled expression on his face. Then I saw a tear form in his eye as he said, "You know, Jim, I wish I'd had the foresight to have a meeting like that while my Gladys was still alive. It would have been so meaningful for her to share with our kids her values and what was really important to her." He paused, grabbed me by both shoulders, looked me straight in the eyes, and said, "I'd love to participate, and I'm honored that your parents have asked me."

I told Mr. Raymond that our meeting would involve sharing information between my parents and the three of us children in four different areas. I showed him the forms we had prepared to summarize that information in a binder we called the "Lifefolio." I asked him if he would be willing to share these forms with my parents. He responded, "I've known Clair and Jim for a long time. I don't think we'll have any trouble putting this together."

I felt very relieved after the visit with Mr. Raymond. I wasn't sure how I was going to approach my parents myself to gather all that information, and he took quite a load off of my mind.

It took me a few weeks to coordinate all of our busy schedules with my parents. Carolyn's initial reaction was, "John, do you think this is going to do any good? You know Mom and Dad. They're not going to give us that kind of information. They're very private people." I explained to her how I had asked Bunker Raymond to facilitate the meeting and gather the information from them. For the first time, I think my sister actually looked at me with an expression of respect. Or at least it seemed that way.

We finally all agreed on the first weekend in April for our meeting. Both Carolyn and John would arrive late in the morning on Saturday, stay overnight, and leave after breakfast on Sunday. But Mom couldn't convince them to stay and go to church with us. She commented, "At least I tried. Neither your brother nor your sister has ever been very interested in church. Thank God at least one of you is religious." I guess she meant that as a compliment to me.

The first Saturday in April finally arrived. As we sat around the dining room table, we looked at each other nervously. I glanced at the old walnut chairs and table that had supported us through so many Christmas and Thanksgiving dinners while we were growing up. Mr. Raymond was at one end, Mom and Dad were huddled together at the other end, and the three of us were sprinkled in between. Mr. Raymond opened with the comment, "I'm so glad you were all able to get together. Your mom and dad were hoping that they would have some way of sitting down with you and sharing with you what was important to them, but they just weren't sure how to do it. Luckily, young Jim came up with the idea of this family meeting. Your parents have spent a lot of time writing down their thoughts and gathering up important information to share with you."

Mr. Raymond continued, "Now before we get started, do any of you have any questions?" My brother glanced at me with a painful look on his face, clearly uncomfortable that he was here with his parents on a Saturday morning and not out on the soccer field cheering his boys on. Carolyn just stared straight ahead stoically. "Okay, let's get started," Mr. Raymond continued. "The first area we want to discuss is 'Values or Life lessons'." This is the section where Clair and Jim Sr. will share with you ideas and values that they feel are important and would like to see continued in the family."

Mom jumped in, "We're not trying to tell the three of you how to run your lives. But we would just like you to know what has been important to us — those values that have helped us — that we think can help you. I know, John and Carolyn, you haven't been active churchgoers, but Dad and I feel that having a spiritual presence in your lives is valuable. We especially think that John, you should bring the boys to Sunday school. I don't mean that they need to be active Methodists like we are, but they should be introduced to religion and God so that they can make their own decisions."

John responded, "I know, Mom, but their soccer schedules are so crazy. We're traveling all over the state almost every weekend. It's impossible to get to church."

Mom looked at him and added, "I know that soccer and sports are so important to you all, but just give them a chance to look and learn. I've heard that the Universalist Church has a great program for kids that doesn't force them into certain beliefs, but gives them a chance to learn about all the world's religions. I'm just asking you to take a look."

"All right, Mom, we can do that." John responded.

Mom then emphasized how important it was to get the whole family together at least twice a year. Since we were young, we had always gotten together at Thanksgiving, and then again for at least a week during the summer at the family cottage on Cape Cod. In recent years, one or two of us hadn't shown up for at least one of the annual events because of business trips or games. The tradition was slowly fading away. Mom was really starting to get warmed up now. "We just can't let the family slip away. After Dad and I are gone, one of you has to make sure the whole family gets together at least twice a year. Otherwise each of you is just

Mom jumped in, "We're not trying to tell the three of you how to run your lives. But we would just like you to know what has been important to us — those values that have helped us — that we think can help you.

going to go your own way and you won't be connected anymore. It's so important to keep the family together. That might not seem so important to you now, but when you get older, you'll see what I mean."

That's when I jumped in. Keeping the family together is really important to me. I've seen too many people wandering around in life with no support system and I didn't want it to happen to us. "Mom, I'll make sure that we get together as a family at least twice a year, no matter what. Certainly we can share Thanksgiving rotating amongst us each year. But getting together at the Cape all depends on whether we still have the cottage." That's when Dad finally spoke up. "That's a very important point, Son. As part of this meeting, we need to make some decisions about the Cape. It may be the most important decision we make today." The room suddenly became very quiet.

Mr. Raymond then changed the direction of the conversation as he looked at the three of us.

"It's important to know what your parents' wishes are for their passing. This is certainly not an easy topic to discuss, but it is an important one." It was clear that my Dad wanted to say something. He sat up straight and cleared his throat. "Your mother and I have thought about this a lot. It hasn't been easy to discuss, but we both realized it was important to deal with. We want you to know that we both expect to be cremated. We don't expect you to spend a lot of money on a casket. So keep it simple. We'd like to be buried next to each other at the cemetery in Walton. That's where my father and mother are. It's a family plot and there's still room for several of us."

He continued, "We'd expect that you'd invite family and friends to a memorial service at the Methodist church, but nothing more than that. We know Reverend Jacobs very well and we trust that he would do a good job. And I guess that's about it."

Dad continued, "I've made a list of where all the important stuff is, the deeds on our two homes, the insurance policies, the titles for the two cars. Most of it is in that green box."

It was very quiet in the room. We looked at each other for what seemed like an eternity until I broke the silence. "Dad, have you seen an estate planning attorney To see if everything is set up properly?"

"No, Son, but Bunker has suggested we meet with Attorney Sperling down on LaSalle Road. He specializes in this kind of stuff."

Mr. Raymond added, "Good point, Jimmy. Your parents not only need to make sure their will is still set up the way they want, but they each have to have a durable power of attorney drafted and a health care proxy."

"What's that?" I responded.

"The durable power of attorney allows someone to make financial decisions for your parents if they are incapacitated. It gives them the opportunity to act on each other's behalf and gives someone else the opportunity to act for them if neither of them is up to it."

My mother added, "We've each got a living will. We've put them in the green metal box in the study with the rest of our important papers, life insurance policies, etc. We certainly don't want to be kept alive if we're just vegetables."

Dad continued, "I've made a list of where all the important stuff is, the deeds on our two homes, the insurance policies, the titles for the two cars. Most of it is in that green box."

My brother, John, had been very quiet for most of the meeting, but was at least beginning to look a little more comfortable. He asked a good question. "What's the health care proxy for? You mentioned that along with the power of attorney."

Mr. Raymond responded, "The health care proxy gives a person the authority to make decisions about your parents' health care if they are not able to. That person carries out the wishes they have stated in their living will. It's an important and sometimes very difficult responsibility. Doctors will look to this person to make medical decisions if your mom and dad can't."

My brother's eyelids were starting to get heavy. No doubt, the topics we were discussing had become mentally draining. Mom looked around the table and said, "I think it's time we all take a break and have some lunch. I've fixed some sandwiches and that chicken noodle soup you all enjoy. Let's eat." As usual Mom was always prepared to feed us. She loved to do it and we didn't complain a bit. Her food was always great. And there was plenty of it.

After a very tasty lunch and some light conversation, we got back to work. Bunker Raymond reassumed his role as our facilitator. His gentle smile and warm tone calmed us all down. He reopened the meeting, "We're now on to discussing those items that your mother and father have that they cherish, those personal items that have emotional value. These are the things that your parents want preserved and passed on to the family members who might appreciate them the most."

Mom was prepared to speak again, "I inherited this beautiful diamond ring from my mother and I want to pass it on to you, Carolyn. This ring will be yours when I'm gone. And John, your wife, Susan, is such a good mother. I'm sure she'd have plenty of uses for my sterling silverware set. I hope she'll put it out when the family celebrates Thanksgiving together. It was a wonderful gift to me from your father on our 25th wedding anniversary. I'll never forget that night." She grabbed my father's hand and squeezed it.

This seemed to be the signal for Dad to talk. "Jim, I've admired your work with your hands for a long time. You seem to be able to fix just about anything and have built some pretty impressive furniture. I'd like you to have my tools. I'm sure they'll get plenty of use in that workshop of yours, especially my table saw and lathe." I thanked him and let him know how much it meant to me.

Mom turned our attention back to her belongings; "I'd like to give my beautiful walnut secretary to my brother Frank's son, Jay. He is such a good boy, and he's always admired that piece of furniture. Please make sure he gets it." We all nodded our heads, almost in unison. "And the rest of my jewelry I'd like to save for my first granddaughter. I don't know which one of you will have a daughter. I hope that's you, Carolyn. I'm sure you would love to have a daughter."

Carolyn blurted out, "Mom, I'm not even married yet and you're thinking about grandchildren already!"

"Well, one day that handsome boyfriend of yours is going to ask you to marry him!" Carolyn's ears turned a bright red.

Dad added one more item, "John, I know how much you love music. I'm not sure what you'll do with all those old 78s and 33s of mine, but I'd like to give them to you."

John was thrilled, "Oh yeah, Dad. That is great! I can download them all onto my iPod. I've got some great software that will take out all the scratches. They'll sound fabulous. It will take awhile, but it will be well worth it. Then I can share it with Carolyn and Jim and we can all enjoy your music forever."

"You know that your mom and I have been pretty private about our savings and investments. We didn't think it was any of your business to know what we have accumulated. But this whole process has got me thinking. Why shouldn't you know?"

For a few moments, the room was silent. I looked up at the clock. It was 2:00 p.m. We had started this meeting four hours ago. I knew we would have to get the meeting wrapped up by around 4:00 p.m. But I also knew we had one more important area to discuss — the cottage on Cape Cod. I was worried it wouldn't go so smoothly.

As if on cue, Dad told us he wanted to run the meeting now. He rose from his chair and stood in front of us. "You know that your mom and I have been pretty private about our savings and investments. We didn't think it was any of your business to know what we have accumulated. But this whole process has got me thinking. Why shouldn't you know? We have nothing to hide. As a matter of fact, I'm pretty proud as to what we've been able to accumulate. We've been lucky enough to never be very much in debt. Our first and only mortgage was on our first home on Highland Avenue. We owed less than $10,000. But since then, we've been able to buy everything for cash — even our cars and our house here on Emerson Road. As a result, we've been able to save a fair amount of money, even though I never got a big salary at work. I've laid it all out here on graph paper, showing the banks, the account numbers, and the terms of the CDs. It adds up to over $700,000."

John interrupted him. "Dad, it's all in CDs? How about stocks or mutual funds?"

Mom responded, "You know your father never really liked the stock market. He didn't want to lose any of the money he worked hard to get."

"But you would earn so much more in good mutual funds," John replied.

"And I could have lost the whole thing!" Dad proclaimed. "You never went through the Great Depression and knew what it was like to have almost nothing. Not for me."

It was clear that conversation was going nowhere. I decided to jump in. "You did a great job putting all that information together, Dad. Where do you keep it?" It was obvious that Dad was proud of his work.

"I've put together a three-ring binder Bunker likes to call my Lifefolio. It's got a section on each important area of our finances, insurance, savings, wills. For all of you, Mom and I will keep this Lifefolio on the bookshelf above the desk in the kitchen."

I was very impressed at how much my father had done to prepare for this meeting. He was really taking this event seriously. He then continued, "Now we need to talk about our real estate. Our home here on Emerson Road is probably worth about $300,000. Although we've lived in it for more than 30 years, we've taken good care of it. It's most likely we'll continue to live here as long as I am alive. Then your mom can decide what she wants to do. When we're gone, you'll probably want to sell it. Is that a fair assumption?"

We all looked at each other for a moment. Carolyn then said, "It's a lovely home, Dad, but none of us are planning to come back and live in town. We've all got our own places."

"Then it's agreed — you'll sell the house," Dad responded, half question, half statement.

John spoke for us, "Yes, Dad that's probably what will happen, unless Mom has sold the house and has used the money to buy a place in a retirement community. Or for that matter if you outlive her, you might do the same."

Dad shook his head. "That's not likely to happen. But let's get on to the big question. What should we do with the Cape Cod cottage?" The cottage had always been the gathering place for the family ever since I could remember. Every summer, my mom would move the family down there when school let out and Dad would spend the weekends with us. Then, when we all went to college, we'd get summer jobs on the Cape and use the cottage as our home base. Now that we were all working, we'd carve out one or two weeks every summer to be there.

"Why don't we kids buy it from you, Dad? We can own it together." I offered.

My brother quickly responded, "That's a great idea, but I don't have any money. I'm saving everything I can for college for the boys."

"Okay, then. Carolyn, you and I can own it. We'll split the costs right down the middle." I knew I couldn't afford it alone on my meager teacher's salary, but with Carolyn's help, I could probably make it work.

But Carolyn wasn't so cooperative. "Jimmy, that would be a nice idea. But I travel so much I'm really not going to get the chance to use the cottage very much. I just don't think it's a good idea for me." And so there we were. Dad suggested, "What if Mom and I give it to you all in the will, and then after we're gone, you can decide how to split it up?" That sounded like a good idea to me. John nodded his head in agreement and Carolyn responded, "That's fine. We'll worry about it then."

Then Bunker Raymond added his thoughts. "I don't want to interfere, but I just don't think that's a good idea. Each of you may have the best of intentions now, but things happen. I had a client at the bank that had a place like yours. When he and his wife passed away, they gave their summer home to their two sons. Well, one son could never come up with the money to pay the taxes. When it was time to clean up the cottage at the beginning or end of the summer season, he was never around. But he was always there for the best weeks of the summer. He treated it like his personal resort hotel. Eventually, his brother became very angry and confronted him. They had a big fight and now they're not talking to each other. It's been three years and neither of them is using the cottage."

It had been a long day, and we had talked about a lot of things — many, frankly, that I thought we would never talk about. It had been difficult getting everyone together, but in the end, it was well worth it.

Then Dad responded, "Jimmy, you seem to be the most interested in keeping the cottage, and you certainly can't afford to buy it from us now. What if we all agreed on its value, gave it to you in the will, and split up the rest of the assets between John and Carolyn? What they get would probably be worth close to the value of the cottage, at least what we have now."

John then posed a question, "That sounds very fair, Dad. But as Mr. Raymond said, things happen. What if you and Mom have to use up your savings for health care? Then there won't be anything left for anyone. Have you thought of that?"

Dad was clearly stumped. The room was silent for quite awhile. Then an idea came to me, "Dad, at school they're offering us a new kind of insurance. It's called long-term care insurance. It covers you if you need care at home or in a nursing home. It picks up where Medicare leaves off."

Dad responded, "I've heard that coverage is awfully expensive. I don't know if we can afford it."

"Well, since we are benefiting from the insurance, what if we helped you pay for it? Does that make sense?" I looked around at everyone in the room.

"I can live with that. What do you think, honey?" He looked at Mom. She nodded her head. I looked over at John and Carolyn.

John said, "Well, I guess we can make it work." Carolyn agreed, but added, "You know the insurance has a medical questionnaire. You have to be in decent health to get it." Mom summed things up. "Fortunately, God has been good to us. We're in very good health for our age. I don't think that will be a problem."

By then, we were all pretty well worn out. It had been a long day, and we had talked about a lot of things — many, frankly, that I thought we would never talk about. It had been difficult getting everyone together, but in the end, it was well worth it. I think my parents had a new sense of comfort. They had laid out their lives before us, and we had responded well. From that day on, family gatherings had a new sense of warmth and closeness. Our family meeting had created a bond that didn't exist before.

The Bottom Line

The family meeting, if conducted properly, will open up the lines of communication between you and your parents and provide them with a feeling of completion and peace of mind. You will have the information you need to make certain that their wishes and desires are met.

The Family Meeting: A Case Study

Chapter 4

Legal Protection for Your Parents

Estate planning is such an ominous term. Most of us try to avoid it as long as possible because it deals with our death and ultimate demise. I would rather we rename it *transition planning*. It is the planning we must do for our parents and ourselves to avoid legal delays and complications when the ownership and/or control of our assets shifts to another person or entity.

I have observed a number of situations where transition planning was not handled properly. The single example that is still vivid in my mind involves one of my clients who was a retired physician. He had gotten married right out of medical school, had three children. He eventually became estranged from his wife and decided to divorce her. Several years later, he remarried and had another two children with his second wife. His second wife was taking care of him when he started to physically and mentally decline. She then decided to place him in a nursing home since she could no longer take care of him at home.

She continued to make decisions regarding his finances, and used their joint checkbook to pay the bills and make purchases while he was in the nursing home. Without warning, the children of the doctor's first wife had an attorney contact her — they contended that she had no authority to make financial decisions on the doctor's behalf even though she was his second and current wife. The family alleged that she was acting irresponsibly and making financial decisions that would result in the depletion of the doctor's assets so that nothing would be left for the children of his first marriage who were still in his will.

Unfortunately, the doctor's second wife had no document that stated she had the right to make financial decisions on his behalf. She was forced to go to probate court to request that she become his *conservator*. A conservator has the legal right to act on behalf of a mentally incompetent individual. She had to testify before the judge that her husband was incompetent — an event that proved very embarrassing for the whole family.

The judge ruled that the doctor could not handle his own affairs, and his second wife was named as his conservator. The whole mess could have been avoided if my client had signed a very short three-page document called a durable power of attorney while he was still healthy. This document gives an individual the right to make financial decisions for you when you are no longer able to make decisions for yourself. A regular power of attorney only allows someone to act on your behalf if you are mentally incompetent. The durable power works regardless of an individual's mental state.

The Documents Your Parents Need

There are several legal documents your parents need to have to avoid legal entanglement, to transfer their assets to whomever they wish, and to make certain their wishes are carried out. These are:

- Will
- Beneficiary statements for life insurance, annuities, and retirement accounts
- Durable power of attorney
- Living will
- Health care proxy
- Possibly one or more trusts

Let's deal with each of these individually.

The Will

First and most well-known document is the *will*. This document states what will happen to your parents' property when they die. If they did not complete a will, they would die "intestate." That means the state in which they reside will decide what happens to their assets. The court will name an executor who will oversee the closing of the estate and charge a healthy fee to do so. In each state, the rules may be different as to who gets what. But one thing is certain — the process will take longer than desired. It will cost more money, and your parents' wishes won't be carried out exactly the way they would want.

You want to be absolutely certain that the will is a legal document in the state that your parents reside. A local attorney will make sure of that.

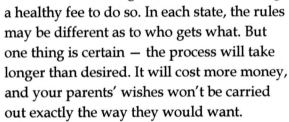

If your parents have never drafted a will, they may resist doing so the first time. Creating a document that states what happens when you die is very final. To set it up, you have to admit that you are actually going to die. One of my clients went through the entire process of planning his estate with an attorney. He and his wife met with the attorney several times and hammered out all the details of who was going to get what.

But a few months later, I got a call from the attorney. He said, "Bob, I still haven't heard back from your client. His unsigned will is sitting on my desk." I called my client, and he made some excuse about not having the time to stop by the attorney's office. He finally signed the will right before he and his wife were flying to Hawaii on vacation. I guess he finally admitted that he could die in a plane crash.

Each of your parents should have their own individual will expressing their personal desires. The will doesn't have to describe what happens to each object that they own, but it should lay out their general wishes with verbiage that perhaps says something like "I leave my tangible property to …" They can attach a *letter of instruction* to the will to identify specific items that they want to go to individuals. This letter of instruction can be changed from time to time without having to redraft the will.

I suggest strongly that they use an attorney to help them draft the will. You want to be absolutely certain that the will is a legal document in the state that your parents reside. A local attorney can make sure of that. I'm sure you have heard of a number of software programs out there that provide the basics of will writing. Unfortunately, you can't be sure that your state would recognize that particular format as legally binding. Don't take the chance. Select an attorney that is familiar with estate planning. Ask your friends and associates if they know a good estate-planning attorney. You don't want to use someone who primarily does real estate closings but only does one or two wills per year.

The Beneficiary Statement

Your parents won't require a will to transfer all their assets. If they own any life insurance policies, annuities, IRAs, or other retirement plans, these investments all pass to the named beneficiary on the beneficiary statement. When your parents set up these accounts, they filled out a beneficiary statement. This beneficiary statement asks them to name primary and contingent beneficiaries. The primary beneficiary is usually their spouse and the contingent is usually their children, divided in some percentage amount amongst them.

It does not matter how your parents have their wills set up. For example, even though your father's will says that everything he has goes to your mom, if his life insurance beneficiary statement indicates that the life insurance proceeds go to his brother, then his brother will get the money.

Make sure your parents maintain a copy of the beneficiary statement for each life insurance policy, IRA, or annuity they have.

First, make sure you can locate the beneficiary statements for each of the accounts I have mentioned. Review the beneficiary statements with your parents. Make sure that is still their wish. If one of your parents is deceased, make sure they are no longer listed as the primary beneficiary for your living parent. In this case, children would move up to primary beneficiaries. Make sure they have both primary and contingent beneficiaries listed on the statement. Then file a copy of these statements away in their Lifefolio. Remember that their will does not have any impact on their IRAs, life insurance policies, annuities, and other retirement plans. Only the beneficiary statement will decide who will get these assets.

Make sure your parents maintain a copy of the beneficiary statement for each life insurance policy, IRA, or annuity they have. If you can't find one, call or write the insurance company, bank, or investment company and ask for a new beneficiary form. If they hold an IRA at a bank that has been bought by another bank, make sure you get an updated statement from the new bank. One of my clients came to me after the very tragic death of both of her parents in an auto accident. She was the contingent beneficiary of their IRAs. Unfortunately, the bank where they had opened their IRAs had been bought and merged into larger banks five times. We only had the original statement showing them as owners of the IRAs. It took us several months to prove to the new bank what had happened. They had no record of the IRAs on their computer. That information had never been transferred over.

Durable Power of Attorney

The third document is the *durable power of attorney*. You may use this document many times. It allows the *attorney-in-fact* to act on your parents' behalf, sign checks for them, sign legal documents, etc. It must be updated every two to three years. At some point, you may hear your mother or dad make a comment that their checkbook is messed up or not accurate. This is a signal that they may be having difficulty keeping up with their financial affairs. Ask them to show you their check register or last monthly bank statement. If you see that duplicate checks were sent to the same source or they hadn't kept up with the balance, it may be time for someone to help them out.

Make sure that your parents also have the durable power of attorney to act in each other's behalf.

Selecting someone to give the power of attorney to is an important decision. That person has control of your parents' money just as they would. It might be a good job for the alpha child — the child that is most comfortable discussing financial affairs with them. But if that child is extremely busy or does not live nearby, then he or she is not a good candidate. Make sure that the individual is extremely trustworthy, patient, and is interested in taking this responsibility. I don't suggest parents give the power of attorney to several of their children. This dilutes the responsibility and culpability of the job. Name one person and possibly one backup as the attorney-in-fact.

Make sure that your parents also have the durable power of attorney to act in each other's behalf. This may sound insignificant, but lacking this document can often cause problems. One of my clients became very ill. He was in the hospital when I called his home to suggest that he transfer an investment from one fund that was performing poorly to a CD with a higher interest rate. He needed to sign a document to make the transfer. If his wife had a durable power of attorney, she could have signed the document for him. She didn't have the authority, so we had to wait until he was well enough to do it himself.

The Living Will

In addition to a will and a durable power of attorney, your parents need to create two documents called *advance directives*. These are legal documents that explain in advance their wishes regarding medical care. The documents also name someone to make medical decisions for them if they are not able to do so. The first of these advance directives is the living will. This document allows your parents to declare what care they desire if they are critically ill. They can specify under what conditions they want to be resuscitated and under what conditions they want to be kept alive.

There are a number of sources for living wills. Most hospitals can provide you with one. Another excellent source is the website www.agingwithdignity.com. They call their version of the living will *"The Five Wishes."* In this document, individuals specify the details regarding their five wishes; these are:

1. Which person you want to make health care decisions for you when you can't make them.

2. The kind of medical treatment you want or don't want.

3. How comfortable you want to be.

4. How you want people to treat you.

5. What you want your loved ones to know.

More that nine million copies of "The Five Wishes" are circulating around the U.S. More than 10,000 organizations, including churches, synagogues, hospices, and doctors' and lawyers' offices, are distributing this unique document.

Another source of state-specific legal living wills is an organization called Choice in Dying. Their phone number is 800-989-9455.

Your parents may have difficulty discussing these subjects, but it's important to get their wishes down on paper. Recently, one of my elderly clients became very ill and had to go to the hospital. She slowly drifted into a coma. I met with her two children. They each had totally different opinions on how she should be treated. One insisted that she not be resuscitated if her heart stopped. The other was adamant about the necessity to keep her alive at all costs. He claimed that miracles can happen and she might fully recover. They almost got into a shouting match at the hospital before I calmed them down. But the decision was beyond their control. She passed away in her sleep a few nights later.

There are a few ways that you can begin the discussions with your parents about their wishes. First, you can put it on the agenda of the family meeting. But if this is very difficult for them to talk about, you might try a more informal approach. If one of their friends or a relative died recently, ask them about the situation. Do they feel the person was treated properly? Would they want to be treated the same? How do they feel about the being kept alive by modern medical technology? Would they want to be resuscitated if they stopped breathing?

This can lead to even deeper discussions about their religious beliefs and possibly their own fears about death. Many elderly people find that they have difficulty sleeping because they are anxious about their own future demise and the circumstances surrounding it. It is usually because they have never candidly discussed their death with anyone and have not made their wishes clear. Take that burden away from them. Give them a chance to share their concerns with you.

The Health Care Proxy

The second advance directive is the *health care proxy*. It is also known as the *health care power of attorney.* "The Five Wishes" includes it as the first wish. However, this form is not approved in every state. The person identified in the health care proxy is equally as important as the person identified in the durable power of attorney. It is this person's responsibility to make certain that the doctors and medical staff honor your parent's wishes as specified in their living will. They may be asked to make life-or-death decisions in very stressful conditions. I suggest that your parents not name more than one child to have this authority. It can often result in heated arguments and hurt feelings. They might be better off not identifying a child but instead a close friend or sibling.

Many elderly people find that they have difficulty sleeping because they are anxious about their own future demise and the circumstances surrounding it.

I was in the hospital standing next to the wife of one of my very best friends when a neurosurgeon asked her if he should operate. He had suffered a massive stroke and was in a coma. The doctor told her that if he did not operate, my friend would most likely die. If he operated, my friend would live, but there was a 50-percent chance he would be a vegetable. The doctor told her she had five minutes to decide. These are the types of decisions the health care proxy must make.

Trusts

The last item to discuss in transition planning is the *trust*. Your parents may have already asked you if you know anything about living trusts. There are a number of law firms and estate planners that promote living trusts in seminars and workshops. Often a living trust is portrayed as the solution to all their concerns. It is very helpful in some cases, but in many others, it is not necessary.

First, let's define what a trust is. It is a legal entity that separates the legal ownership of property from the beneficial ownership of property. In a trust, one person or a group of persons (the *trustees*) hold assets (the *corpus*) for the benefit of one or more other people (the *beneficiaries*). The person who creates the trust by transferring his or her money, property, or assets to the trustee is the *grantor* or *settlor* of the trust. The terms and conditions of the trust are specified in the *trust document*. It is the trustee's job to make sure that the provisions of the trust are carried out in accordance with the wishes of the grantor as stated in the trust document. The trustee has a very important role (described as a *fiduciary responsibility*): to make sure the terms of the trust are followed.

Your parents should consider a living trust if they have a number of different investments, property in another state, or a very complicated financial situation.

There are essentially two types of trusts: *living trusts* and *testamentary trusts*. The living trust is an *intervivos trust* which means it is set up during the grantor's lifetime, and it is effective while they are alive. A testamentary trust is created by your parents' will and does not take effect until they die. Your parents might use a living trust to hold all their assets like real estate, stocks, and bonds. They could name each other or themselves as trustee of the living trust and name someone else as a successor trustee.

There are several advantages to the living trust:

- Assets held in a living trust go directly to the beneficiary when the grantor (your parent) dies and does not go through the delay and cost of the probate court process.

- In the event of your parent's incapacity, the trustee (if not your parent) or the successor trustee (if your parent is a trustee) can take over management of trust property smoothly and immediately.

- Property held in another state (if part of the living trust) does not have to go through probate court in that state.

- Living trusts can be revoked, changed, or funded at any time during your parents' lifetime.

- All types of assets can be put into the trust and managed as one entity.

Since the living trust is revocable, it can be changed; assets owned by the trust are still part of your parents' estate and are included for any estate or succession taxes due to the state or federal government.

Your parents should consider a living trust if they have a number of different investments, property in another state, or a very complicated financial situation. The living trust is like a big basket. All their assets can be placed in it and protected from the time-consuming probate court process. Each of your parents should have their own living trust, holding their share of the assets. They can control it themselves and can pass on control to a successor trustee if they are no longer capable. The successor trustee does not need a durable power of attorney.

The living trust can become a testamentary trust at your parents' death. That means it becomes irrevocable or unchangeable at that time. Let us assume that your father had a living trust with $1 million worth of assets in it. At his death, his trust becomes *testamentary* (irrevocable). It could then be identified as a family trust with income available to your mother and your children as the ultimate beneficiaries of the assets. As a result of this irrevocable status, the assets in this trust would not be included in your mother's estate and would avoid any potential estate or succession tax at her death.

Assets are often shifted to *irrevocable trusts* to remove them from a person's estate. Once this is done, the assets cannot be shifted back to the individual without tax consequences. Using trusts is a complicated process. It is important to use a good estate-planning attorney to set up and administer this type of legal vehicle. But it can be very beneficial to your parents in reducing potential taxes, reducing the delay in processing their estates, and making sure that their wishes are carried out.

Testamentary Trusts

Testamentary trusts carry out the wishes of donors after they die. The most popular form of testamentary trust is the *credit shelter trust*. Sometimes known as the *marital trust*, this trust receives assets from the donor at their death equal to the amount of assets that are sheltered from estate taxes. A surviving spouse can receive income from this trust, but is limited in utilizing any of the principal. As a result, the money that goes into the credit shelter trust is not taxed by the federal government and is not included in the surviving spouse's estate.

Another use of a testamentary trust is to make certain that mentally or physically challenged children are taken care of. This type of trust is called a *special needs trust*. If a parent passes away and there is no surviving spouse to take care of a disabled child, this trust is set up to make certain that the child is taken care of. A trustee is named who watches over the funds and uses them for the child's benefit. This same type of trust can be used to take care of aging parents if you predecease them.

The Bottom Line

If you implement the legal tools that I have discussed in this chapter, your parents will avoid most of the legal pitfalls that they can encounter during their lives. It would be very wise for you to implement these same tools for yourself as well. These legal tools can protect your family from a great deal of unneeded expense, unwanted delays, and unnecessary frustration. If you select the right attorney, these documents can be set up at a reasonable cost and will give you and your family much more control over the financial hurdles that you will face.

Chapter 5
Transferring Real Estate

If you have a chance to review your parents' assets, you will probably find that their home is their most valuable investment. Many of our parents bought their homes for a price one-tenth of what they are worth today. If they grew up during the Depression, your parents probably don't have a mortgage either. They may have saved up and paid cash for their house or paid off their traditional mortgage years ago.

In addition to the family home, some of our parents were able to buy a vacation home at a beautiful location such as Cape Cod, Montana, Florida, or Arizona. These properties have grown in value even more than their primary home. In many cases, they have become a family gathering place where parents, children, and grandchildren can all get together and relax.

In many cases, our parents have no idea how to divide up their real estate. Since they are not sure what to do, they'll often leave it to their children to decide amongst themselves after they are gone. This is a recipe for disaster. Most likely, not every child will have the same interest in keeping the property. One might want to sell it; one might want to keep it but has no interest in helping to pay its ongoing costs. And of course, all the grandchildren want to keep the property since it often has been such a place of joy for them.

> *If you have a chance to review your parents' assets, you will probably find that their home is their most valuable investment.*

How are you to advise your parents to plan for the disposition of their property in a way that you and your siblings have a say in it? To do it properly often involves several professionals, but it is well worth it. How would you put a value on your brother's unwillingness to talk to you for the last 10 years because he feels cheated that you didn't listen to his suggestions about selling of the property? You, your siblings, and your parents must discuss with professional advisors all the options available to your parents in transferring the value of their real estate or risk the potential impact on the family.

Let's look at various options and see how they might work. Here's an example: I had a client with substantial investment assets as well as a beautiful colonial home in a very nice suburban town. In his family meeting, he learned that one of his three children was very interested in living in the family home. It was in an excellent school system and was just right for this son's growing family. My client decided to leave his home to that child after he and his wife passed away and left a comparable amount of investments and other property to the other two children to balance it out.

That scenario works if your parents have accumulated significant investments in addition to the house. But what if they haven't and they still want to give the house to one child? Your parents could purchase a second-to-die life insurance policy for an amount comparable to the value of the house and make those children not receiving the house the beneficiaries. A second-to-die policy would pay the death proceeds only when the second parent passed away. One child would get the house and the other two would get tax-free cash equal to its value.

You, your siblings, and your parents must discuss with professional advisors all the options available to your parents in transferring the value of their real estate or risk the potential impact on the family.

Gifting Real Estate Before Death

But what if your parents want to give their home to one of their children now rather than wait until they have passed away? One of my clients came to me and said that his mother had transferred the ownership of her home to him. She did this to get it out of her estate and protect it from the state if she should need nursing home care. She still intended to live in the house for the rest of her life. Unfortunately, she had already made the transfer, so there was nothing we could do to reverse it, but I told him the reasons why she shouldn't have made that move. First of all, she transferred the cost basis of her home to her son. She and his father had bought the home for $37,000 in 1955. It was recently appraised for $550,000. All the gain in the house would be taxable when her son sold the house in the future. If she had passed the house to him after her death, all the gain would have been forgiven for tax purposes. This forgiveness of gain is called *step up in basis* and would apply to any capital property like stocks and real estate.

In addition, the house was now a potential target for the son's creditors. That might not concern him but it should concern his mother. If he should ever have credit problems, the creditors could attach their loans to the house and potentially drive her out and sell the house right out from under her. Also, if her son had marital problems and got divorced, his ex-wife could claim the house as one of the assets in the divorce settlement. All in all, the direct gift of a parent's home to you is not a good idea.

A better approach would have been for my client's mother to retain a *life interest* in her home and gift the remainder or future interest in the house to her son. This is called a *life estate*. Two entities, the *life tenant* and the *remainderman*, hold title to the property. The life tenant has the right to use the property for life, and the remainderman obtains the ownership of the property at the death of the life tenant. The life tenant pays the cost of the property while she is alive. She avoids her child's creditors and potential ex-spouse. Another benefit is that the property does not have to go through the probate process at her death, simplifying the transfer and reducing the cost.

The life tenant retains any of the tax benefits of owning the house, and most importantly, the life estate is not a completed gift until the mother dies. That means the son can take advantage of the step up in basis and avoid potentially big capital gains taxes when he eventually sells the house.

With the life estate, the gift of the home is not complete until the parent dies. That means the value of the home is still included in her estate at death. If the house is worth a great deal, this could significantly impact the estate taxes due to the federal and state government. When the probate court reviews all the assets in your parent's estate, the home would be included. The amount of estate and succession tax paid to the state and federal government is based on the size of this estate. The larger it is, the more tax may have to be paid. If a parent wants to reduce their potential estate tax, they can do so by using a *qualified personal residence trust (QPRT)*.

A qualified personal residence trust is an irrevocable (unchangeable) trust set up by your parents. When they put their home into the trust, it becomes a permanent (irrevocable) gift to the beneficiaries of the trust, who are usually one or more of the children. But this is not an immediate gift. When the trust is set up, it is set up with a time limit. The longer the time limit, the smaller the gift to the trust.

For example, if your father as donor was to transfer a $1 million residence to a QPRT, retaining the right to use the residence for a seven-year term, the value of the present gift to the remainder beneficiaries (the children) might be only 50 percent or $500,000. If your father survives the seven-year term, the residence will not be included in his estate for tax purposes, nor will any of the appreciation in value of the residence occurring after the initial transfer. If, after seven years, the residence has appreciated in value to $1.4 million, the parents will have succeeded in transferring this amount to their children at the same tax cost as a transfer of only $500,000.

In order for the trust to work, the donor (your father) must live the full seven years. Otherwise, the house reverts to their estates and there is no gift. But if he does survive, this is a great tool to give the house to the children for a much-reduced estate cost. Your parents can still live in the house for those seven years and get all the tax benefits of home ownership during that period of time. If they wish to remain in the house after the trust term has ended, they will have to pay rent to the beneficiaries of the trust (the children) to avoid any IRS question of an incomplete gift.

Unique Real Estate Considerations

What if one of your brothers or sisters has chosen to stay at home to take care of your parents? You certainly wouldn't want to sell the house and leave them homeless when your parents died. You would probably want to reward them for being willing to take on that responsibility. Your parents could state in their will that your sibling could stay in the house for the rest of his or her life, but at his or her death, the house would be sold and the proceeds divided amongst the families of all the children. This would reward the caregiving child, as well as ultimately share the inheritance equally.

I had a client who had four children. None of them indicated in the family meeting that they were certain they wanted to buy their parents' home, but they wanted to ability to do so in the future. They didn't want the sale of the house to be automatic when their parents passed away. They agreed with their parents to set up an option program. When their parents were gone, they agreed that a firm they were all familiar with would make an appraisal. That appraised value would be the price any of them had the option to exercise to buy the house. The option period would only be open for one year after their parents' death. If none of the children had exercised the option by then, the house would be sold and the proceeds shared equally. All the children thought this solution would be fair. I agree. No one child had any distinct advantage over any other. They all have the opportunity to buy the

If your parents own rental property or some type of property that generates significant income, the situation can become more complex.

house if they choose to at a price established by an objective third party. The only limitation is that they have a limited time to make the decision. The executor of the estate has to put a time limit on the sale because he or she needs to dispose of the house to settle the estate. It gave the children the flexibility of buying the house in the future without having to make a decision now.

In this case, if more than one of the children wished to buy the house, it could be handled in two different ways. The sale could go to the highest bidder or the children could create a partnership agreement spelling out each of their responsibilities and buy the home as partners. It would be much simpler, however, if only one of them purchased the house.

If your parents own rental property or some type of property that generates significant income, the situation can become more complex. Some of the children may wish to keep the investment property and some might just want to sell it to get the cash. One of the ways to make an illiquid real estate investment more liquid so the children have various options is to create a *family limited partnership*.

One of my clients owned a very profitable motel. By just overseeing the staff of the motel and working two or three days a week, he received a very handsome income. He decided he wanted to give his children the opportunity to keep the property and continue to receive a nice income. So he created a family limited partnership. He placed the motel in the partnership. He and his wife became general partners of the partnership and his three sons became limited partners. Each of the partners owns a certain number of shares in the partnership.

In the beginning, my client and his wife owned all the shares, since they had owned the property. But over time, they gifted shares in the partnership to their children. Thus, over the years, they transferred the ownership of the property to their children. Each child will own a certain number of shares in the partnership and can buy out his partners in the future. If one of the sons wants to maintain the property and receive the income, he can buy out his brothers. Or all three brothers could hire someone to run the property and receive the income based on the number of shares they own. The benefit of this solution is that the children have a choice.

The Bottom Line

Planning for the transfer of your parents' real estate is one of the most important things a family can do. If parents and children talk to each other and know each other's needs and concerns, the valuable real estate can benefit the entire family. But if family members don't plan together, this same valuable real estate can become the wedge that drives the family apart. That's why it's so important to invest the time and effort in working with a professional to create a real estate plan that works for your family.

Chapter 6
Investing Your Parents' Assets

Most of the parents of Baby Boomers have very conservative investment portfolios. Traditionally, they have invested their money in CDs, savings accounts, and savings bonds. Most families have not ventured into the stock market due either to their concern about risk or lack of knowledge. This approach probably served them well in the 1970s and 1980s when interest rates were much higher. But in today's market — when interest rates are at a 40-year low — they can barely squeeze out a 5-percent return from most conservative investments.

This may not be a problem for them, but if they need income from their investments, it can make things very difficult. Let's assume that your parents are in the 28-percent tax bracket. That means that 28 percent of the last dollar they take in from their pension or interest on bank accounts and CDs will go to the federal government. In addition, let's assume that inflation continues at a modest 2 percent. If your parents are earning 5 percent on their investments, 28 percent of that return, or 1.4 percent, will go to taxes. That leaves net earnings of 3.6 percent. If inflation continues at 2 percent, their real earnings are 1.6 percent on their investment.

If you add together the need to provide income for a longer retirement with the need for growth to offset inflation and taxes, you have a formula for disaster if investment planning is not considered.

In addition to this low net rate of return, there is no growth built in to their portfolio. I am sure that they are very aware of what has happened to the prices of groceries, health care, utilities, and gasoline to run their car. Their portfolio must have some growth investments to offset this creeping increase.

Also, your parents are probably going to live a lot longer than their parents. The miracles of modern medicine have produced cures for many diseases that were fatal in the past. Even various forms of cancer have become chronic illnesses rather than terminal diseases. If you add together the need to provide income for a longer retirement with the need for growth to offset inflation and taxes, you have a formula for disaster if investment planning is not considered.

But before you determine that your parents need to reposition their investments, you need to do a little homework. You've got to take a look at their overall situation.

Take Stock of Expenses and Income

First of all, you must work with them to clarify their current financial needs. If your parents are anything like mine, they probably have a very conservative lifestyle and don't spend a great deal of money. But it's important to determine their monthly living expenses.

Divide your parents' expenses into two categories: fixed expenses and discretionary expenses. *Fixed expenses* are those that must be paid each month. They include real estate taxes, utility bills, food, medical expenses, insurance, mortgages, and any other expense necessary for them to live normally. *Discretionary expenses* include items like cable television, subscriptions, travel, vacations, hobbies, and other items that are not essential.

Secondly, you need to determine their sources of income. Many retirees from previous generations have guaranteed pensions from their employers. Most companies have since done away with these pensions due to their cost. In most cases, the only employers still providing guaranteed pensions are the federal, state, and municipal governments, but your parents may be lucky enough to be amongst those who have a guaranteed retirement income. Many are probably receiving a monthly benefit from Social Security as well.

When you determine their recurring monthly income from pensions and Social Security, you need to take into account what will happen when one of your parents dies. Most likely, the pension the family receives will be reduced by a certain percentage, and in some extreme cases, it will stop altogether. This change in pension income is based upon the decision they made when your mother or father retired. They selected a pension option that provided a certain amount of income if they both were alive and a reduced amount when one of them died.

Their Social Security income will also be affected. If your father was the breadwinner, he is receiving a Social Security benefit based upon his contributions to the system during his working years. He may be receiving upwards of $2,000 a month. Your mother will receive an amount based on her working income or half your father's benefit; whichever is higher. Likewise, the same situation could be reversed. If your mother was the primary breadwinner, her Social Security income will be higher, and your father can choose his benefit or half of hers.

In any case, if the primary Social Security recipient dies, the surviving spouse then continues to get their current benefit or 100 percent of the deceased spouse's benefit, whichever is higher.

In addition to a pension and Social Security, if your mother or father served in the military and maintained reserve status for 20 years or more, they are probably receiving a military retirement benefit. This retirement benefit, along with Social Security, increases each year based upon a cost-of-living factor. When my father retired, his military benefit was approximately the same as his pension. But after 20 years, his military pension was twice as much as his company pension due to the increases based on the cost of living. People who are fortunate enough to retire from those companies with a cost-of-living factor built in to their pension are very lucky, and they will receive a benefit far more than their original fixed pension if they live 20 years or more in retirement.

Generate More Income

Now that you have determined what your parents' monthly expenses are and what their guaranteed income is, you will see if there is a gap between the two. Ideally, these guaranteed sources of income should be enough to cover their fixed expenses, but this is not always the case. Do their total expenses exceed their monthly guaranteed income? If so, by how much? Let's say your parents' total monthly expenses are $3,500. They are receiving $1,500 from Social Security and $1,000 from a company pension. In years past, that was enough to cover expenses, but your father's company has discontinued paying for retirees' health

In addition to a pension and Social Security, if your mother or father served in the military and maintained reserve status for 20 years or more, they are probably receiving a military retirement benefit.

benefits and your parents now require a part-time health aide. As a result, their expenses have increased by $1,000 a month, so their investments need to safely produce this additional $1,000 per month.

The next step is to determine how we can produce this additional $1,000 per month. What are their total investments and savings? Let's say your parents have $50,000 in a CD, $25,000 in savings bonds, $50,000 in a traditional savings account, and $25,000 in stocks. The CD may be producing a 5-percent income; the savings bonds 4 percent, the savings account 3 percent, but the stocks are only paying a 2-percent dividend. The total income from these three sources is $4,750 per year, far below their requirement of $12,000.

Your parents will have to do one of two things in this situation — either reduce their expenses so that their current investments can cover the gap or change their mix of investments to produce a greater return. Let's assume that they can't reduce their expenses below the current level. This means we will have to find a way to produce $12,000 per year from their $150,000 of investments. That's a return of 8 percent.

At the time of this writing, it certainly doesn't look possible to find any investments that can consistently produce an 8-percent return without a great deal of risk. Therefore we will have to take a different approach. One alternative is a systematic withdrawal method. This is the method used by large institutions, such as colleges and universities, to produce consistent income over a long period of time. These institutions have learned that if they have a mix of investments made up of 60 percent stocks and 40 percent bonds and they systematically withdraw the same amount from this pool of investments each month, they can produce a better income for a longer period of time than just a portfolio of bonds or CDs.

A study by Fidelity Investments shows that if a retired couple had $500,000 to invest in 1972, and they invested the portfolio in 50 percent stocks, 40 percent bonds, and 10 percent short-term investments and withdrew 5 percent of the portfolio each year, their investments would last 27 years. If they withdrew 6 percent a year, their portfolio would last 21 years. At an 8-percent withdrawal rate, their portfolio would last 15 years.

In our example, if your parents reallocated their investments into a portfolio of mutual funds with 50 percent of the $150,000 in stock mutual funds, 40 percent in bond mutual funds, and 10 percent in money market funds or CDs, they could begin to withdraw $1,000 a month from this portfolio and expect it to last approximately 15 years. Of course, there is no guarantee that it will last this long. Market conditions and the selection of funds could shorten or lengthen the period that the money would last.

A second alternative would be to utilize an *immediate annuity* to produce the $1,000 per month. An immediate annuity is a product offered by insurance companies. With a traditional immediate annuity, your parents would transfer a lump sum to the insurance company to provide a guaranteed income to them for the rest of their lives. This alternative would eliminate the risk of investing in stocks to produce their income, but it would have two disadvantages. First, they no longer would have access to their principal investment since they transferred it to an insurance company. Second, the income would be fixed and could not increase to offset inflation.

However, the insurance industry has produced a new form of immediate annuity that is much more attractive than the traditional immediate annuity. It is known as an *immediate variable annuity*. The insurance company offers a monthly income that is based on your parent's life expectancy. That income can go up if the underlying investments your parents have chosen go up. The income is guaranteed not to go below a certain level known as the *guaranteed minimum income*. In addition, during a certain period of time, known as the *access period* (usually 20 years), your parents can still access their principal.

This form of immediate variable annuity eliminates all the objections most people have to buying an annuity. Their income is not fixed but can increase. They have access to their principal for a period of time, and they have a number of investment options to choose from. The primary objection most people have to this new form of annuity is its cost. The total underlying costs of such an annuity are generally 2.5 to 3 percent per year. In comparison, the typical mutual fund's annual cost is generally 1 to 1.5 percent.

Investing Your Parents' Assets

Using Their Home's Equity

What will your parents do if the investment strategies you have chosen for them still don't produce enough income or if they don't have any significant investments at all? If they own a home, there is still hope. That is, if they own a home that doesn't have a big mortgage. Most likely if they have lived in their house a long time, they have paid off most of the debt, and the house has gone up in value substantially. As a result, substantial equity has been built up in the house.

The key is to find a way to unlock this equity to provide an income for your parents. One of my clients had a similar problem. She had been retired for over 10 years from her job as an executive secretary at a large insurance company. She had a small pension and Social Security to provide most of her income. In addition, she had approximately $100,000 in investments to provide an income for her. She had chosen to live in a lovely beachfront community near her children. She loved her condo and the town she lived in. Unfortunately, two of her major expenses began to increase substantially. Her condo fee increased from $150 to over $300 per month and her property tax doubled over a period of five years. This lovely community needed more tax money to build all the new schools necessary to meet the needs of new families moving in. She found that her pension, Social Security, and investment income was about $1,000 a month less than her expenses.

The insurance industry has produced a new form of immediate annuity that is much more attractive than the traditional immediate annuity.

My client debated whether she should sell the condo and move into something less expensive. Her son offered to build an addition on his house so she could live there. But she really wanted to stay in her beautiful home, and she wanted to maintain her independence. Fortunately, over the 10 years she had owned her condo, its value had increased substantially and she had no mortgage on the property. We determined that her condo was worth more than $250,000. All that money was locked up in her real estate and wasn't producing any income at all for her.

We first considered applying for a home equity loan. She could get a home equity loan based on the value of the property alone without having to prove her income. The rates were slightly higher than if she could prove adequate income. With a home equity loan, she would have access to this pool of money. She could write checks against it, as she needed it to pay her expenses. The monthly costs of the home equity loan would be an interest charge on the balance borrowed. There were no closing costs or bank charges to set it up. However, the monthly interest charges could change every month as she drew more money out or if the interest rate increased. The interest rate was not fixed but floated as the prime rate changed.

My client didn't like this idea. She didn't want to have the burden of an additional monthly expense — an expense that wasn't locked in that could increase as interest rates changed — even though it freed up over $200,000 for her use. So we had to seek out another alternative. We considered a reverse mortgage.

Reverse Mortgages

A *reverse mortgage* is a loan against your home that you do not have to repay as long as you live there. You can receive the money from a reverse mortgage in a number of different ways: a monthly check, a lump sum, a credit line, or a combination of these choices. Nothing has to be paid back on the loan until you die, move, or sell your home. To be eligible for a reverse mortgage, you must be at least 62 and own your own home.

With a regular mortgage, you normally have to prove your income, and you make payments every month to reduce the debt and increase your equity. A reverse mortgage

A reverse mortgage is a loan against your home that you do not have to repay as long as you live there.

works just the opposite; you don't have to prove your income and you don't make any payments — the mortgage is based on a percentage of the equity in your home. This is the amount available to you. As you receive payments, the debt increases and the equity goes down unless the value of the house increases more than the money you take out.

Reverse mortgages are offered by a number of different organizations. Home Equity Conversion Mortgages (HECM) are federally insured and backed by the U.S. Department of Housing and Urban Development. Other reverse mortgages are offered by private organizations, and in some cases, by state and local government agencies.

The amount you can receive in a reverse mortgage is based on a number of factors: your age, the appraised value of your home, where you live, and how you want to receive the money.

The costs of reverse mortgages are more than regular mortgages. There is generally a substantial up-front fee payable to the provider of the mortgage, similar to points in a regular mortgage. The costs of federally insured reverse mortgages (HECMs) are generally less expensive than those offered by private firms, but the private firms will loan more money to people with larger homes.

After much thought and consideration, my client chose to take out a reverse mortgage. Before she was able to take out the loan, she had to sit with a counselor from an independent government-approved housing counseling agency. The counselor explained to her all the advantages and disadvantages of such a loan. She set up her loan so that she received a monthly check to supplement her income. She and her children know that when she dies or sells the condo, the loan will have to be paid from the proceeds of the sale.

Managing Your Parents' Investments

If your parents are fortunate enough not to need income from their investments, they will have more flexibility in their investment program. Assuming they want to pass on their wealth to the family, their investments can be invested more with growth in mind. This means that their portfolio should be invested at least 60 percent in stocks or stock funds. Such a growth-oriented portfolio involves more risk and needs to be watched more closely.

If your parents have a portfolio that is heavily weighted toward stocks, you should recommend to them that they consider hiring a registered investment advisor to manage their portfolio. In many cases, one of your parents has managed this portfolio for a number of years, and they may be very good at it. Let's assume that your mother or father has been interested in the stock market, has traded his or her own stocks for a number of years, and has done very well.

In many cases, your other parent might not have had a great deal of interest in the stock market. What if something happened to your investor parent and your other parent was left with a portfolio that he/she couldn't manage and knew very little about? He or she then would look to you or one of your siblings to manage the portfolio. Don't be put in this position. Even if your parents don't want anyone outside the family to manage the portfolio right now, help them select someone to take over management if they are no longer able to handle it. They certainly should be willing to do that.

Do not let your parents keep their stock certificates at home.

As I mentioned, suggest that your parents use a registered investment advisor. This is a professional money manager who manages portfolios for a fee. He does not receive commissions for each trade, but charges a flat fee to manage the investments. In this way, you will know that he is not motivated to make a lot of trades to make money. As the portfolio grows, he will make more money because his flat fee will grow. Thus his goal is the same as your parents — to make the portfolio grow and not to make a lot of buys and sells just to generate commissions.

One final thing: do not let your parents keep their stock certificates at home. In many cases, if they bought stock, rather than hold the certificates in a brokerage account, they might have had them mailed to them and retained them at home. This is a recipe for disaster. Stock certificates are just like cash. If someone else gets hold of the certificates, they can redeem them for full value. If the certificates are lost, it is very expensive to replace them. If the stock is worth $10,000, for example, it will cost $200 to $300 to replace the certificate. Also, if the company merged with another company or the stock name changed, your parents' certificates might not have been replaced or updated. If the stock split, they might not have been issued new shares as a result of the split.

All of these problems can be solved if your parents transfer their stocks into a brokerage account. They will no longer have to keep track of the certificates. If there are any mergers or acquisitions, the changes are automatically made to their holdings. If the stock splits, they are automatically issued new shares.

If your parents pass away and they hold individual stock certificates, the executor has to notify each company to change the name of registration over to their estate. But if the stocks are all in a brokerage account, changing the registration of the account itself will re-register all the stocks and each will not have to be changed individually. It saves a great deal of time for the executor.

The Bottom Line

If you have any concerns about your parents' investments, it is best to seek professional help to answer their questions and give them advice. Don't be put in a position to have to help your parents make investment decisions without professional advice. Seek out a certified financial planner or registered investment advisor to help you.

Chapter 7
Long-Term Care
Alternatives for Your Parents

One of the greatest risks to your parent's security is the possibility of one of them suffering a long-term chronic illness. Modern medical science has done wonders to reduce the loss of life due to cancer, heart disease, and other ailments. But as a result, one of your parents (or possibly both) may need some form of care for a long period of time.

According to a study done by the National Institute of Health, an estimated 37 million Americans were age 65 or older in 2006. That is 12 percent of the population. In 2030, it is estimated that 71.5 million people or 20 percent of the population will live to be over 65. The largest growing segment of the American population is the group age 85 or older.

If your parents get sick and spend at least three days in a hospital, their physician can refer them to a nursing home or rehab center to recover. As their care is focused on rehabilitation (skilled care), Medicare will cover the expenses incurred. Medicare will cover up to 100 days in a rehab facility. But currently, Medicare provides limited care for expenses incurred for rehabilitation if your parent chooses to go home. Medicare covers up to 35 hours a week of skilled nursing care and home health aide services. Your parent

One of the greatest risks to your parent's security is the possibility of one of them suffering a long-term chronic illness.

may receive additional hours of skilled physical and occupational therapy and other social services. The amount of care allowed in the plan of care depends on the recommendation of your parent's doctor. Realistically, based on what Medicare pays the home health care agencies, your parent can expect to receive about 10 hours of care per week. Services and supplies approved in the plan of care are covered in full. Durable medical equipment is covered at 80 percent of the Medicare-approved amount. As long as your parent continues to qualify for rehabilitation, there is no time limit on the Medicare benefit. But please note: Medicare will not cover chronic or custodial care if your parent is not expected to recover. Your parent's doctor generally makes that determination.

What do you do if your parent continues to need care after 100 days in a rehab facility? You can leave him in the facility, where he can incur costs of up to $300 a day or more, or you can bring him home. Once he is home, you have three choices. You can expect your other healthy parent to act as caregiver. If this isn't feasible, you, your spouse, or one of your siblings can step in and act as the caregiver. The third choice is to hire a home health care agency to provide care on a daily, weekly, or monthly basis.

In-Home Care

The cost of a health care worker in your parents' home is approximately $15 to $20 an hour in most areas of the country. You may be able to find someone less expensive if you are very lucky, but you would have to hire them directly and not through an agency. The advantage of using the agency is that they have done some background checks on their workers, and

As a result of caregiving for a long period of time, the healthy parent may become a second sick parent.

they usually have the resources to provide you with another person if the first one doesn't work out. If you hire someone directly, you take responsibility for his or her character.

If your healthy parent is required to become the caregiver for your sick parent, it can put a very heavy burden on them. One of my clients had a stroke at age 70. He is a very big man who was an active golfer, but he lost all the strength and movement in his right side. His wife chose to take care of him at home. She was not able to get him in and out of bed by herself, so she hired an aide to come in the morning and to come again at night. For the rest of the day, she acted as his caregiver. As a result, she has been homebound and unable to take any trips or visit any friends for the last five years. She limits her time away from the home to one or two hours per day to shop for groceries or run errands.

As a result of caregiving for a long period of time, the healthy parent may become a second sick parent. Generally, caregivers provide care for their spouse for an average of four to five years. Twenty-two percent of these spousal caregivers suffer from depression. As a result, many families have asked a daughter or the spouse of one of the sons to become a caregiver to the sick parent. This puts an added burden on the family. It is even more difficult if both parents are not well and there is no family member nearby to act as the caregiver. In these cases, if the parents want to stay in the home, a professional aide must be hired.

Alternatives to Home Care

There are certainly other options to staying in the family home. Every week, there are new facilities being built to provide residences for our elderly parents. Some of them are quite nice. My mother is in a retirement community that offers people a number of choices. They can live in freestanding condos or in one or two-bedroom apartment units. In each case, they buy their own unit. When they leave or die, their family is returned 90 percent of the purchase cost. The residents are provided all meals in a common dining room, cleaning services, medical care, numerous social activities, and local van transportation.

If at any time they need more substantial care, they can move to an assisted-living unit. Here they still have their own small apartment, but they are provided with 24-hour care. In addition to the cost of buying a condo or apartment, a monthly fee is charged for all other services. This fee increases substantially if the individual needs to move to assisted care.

In other similar retirement communities, your parents could rent a unit rather than buy it. Renting provides a much lower initial cost, but the monthly fees are usually higher. Many facilities have variations of these two approaches (rent versus buy) that can adjust the total cost up or down. You need to look at each option carefully to see which is best for your parents. Your parents might have the option to purchase a unit that will return 90 percent of the purchase price to them or their heirs if they leave or die. In some cases, they could choose to give up this repurchase guarantee over a seven-year period and, as a result pay, significantly lower monthly charges. If it's more important to keep the costs down, this approach works well. The family needs to understand, though, that they will eventually give up what their parents paid for the unit.

The federal government has put severe restrictions on qualification for Medicaid.

Medicaid and Long-Term Care

How can Medicaid pay for your parents' extensive health care costs? Medicaid is a program jointly funded by the federal and state governments. Each state manages its own program. Medicaid is designed to provide assistance to the indigent. A third of the payments from Medicaid provide payments for the elderly who are in nursing homes. Other funds are provided for those who are disabled or without financial resources. Medicaid does not currently provide any benefits for assisted living or home care. It is strictly for those individuals who are in a nursing home.

In the past, a number of families transferred assets from their parents to other family members to qualify them for Medicaid assistance. Parents transferred their homes, investments, and savings accounts to their children and then applied for Medicaid.

Unfortunately, the number of the elderly applying for Medicaid has increased so much in recent years that it has become a very substantial part of most states' budgets.

As a result, the federal government has put severe restrictions on qualification for Medicaid. Monthly income limits differ depending on whether the applicant is single or married. For a married couple, the spouse remaining in the community (*community spouse*) can retain all of his or her income. The community spouse's income would not be counted in determining the applicant's eligibility for Medicaid. However, all of the applicant's income must be counted for his or her long-term care except for certain deductions. These deductions may include a personal need allowance not to exceed $60 per month (less in some states), an allowance for a dependant child living at home and, depending on the community spouse's income, a portion of the spouse's income for living expenses known as the *minimum monthly maintenance needs allowance (MMMNA)*. In 2008, this amount ranges from $1,711 to a high of $2,610 per month.

If the community spouse's income is less than the MMMNA, a portion of the applicant's income may be used to meet that minimum. The balance will go to the nursing home that provides the care. If the applicant is single, he or she cannot exceed Medicaid income limits and qualify. The limit for 2008 is approximately $1,911 per month but varies from state to state.

To qualify for medicaid coverage, the recipient's countable assets cannot exceed $2,000. The community spouse of the Medicaid recipient may keep half of the couple's joint assets up to $104,400 (in 2008). In any case, the community spouse may keep the first $20,880 (in 2008), even if it exceeds half of the couple's assets. These figures vary from state to state.

Countable assets consist of all investments such as stocks, bonds, mutual funds, checking and savings accounts, and CDs. Countable assets also include any personal or real property as well as any art and collectibles.

Non-countable assets consist of personal possessions such as clothing, jewelry, and furniture and the applicant's primary residence. Further, non-countable assets include one vehicle not to exceed $4,500 for unmarried applicants (there is no value limit for a vehicle for married applicants). Non-countable assets also include prepaid funeral plans, certain amounts of life insurance and retirement funds which cannot be cashed in because they are in payment status (however the latter will be considered under the income limits).

Based on these restrictions, it is very difficult for most people to qualify for Medicaid unless they have already used up their assets to pay for care. But the income restrictions usually exclude most people from being accepted into the program.

Be Careful with Gifts

The federal government has made it extremely difficult for a family to attempt to transfer assets away from their parents to qualify for Medicaid. The sick parent must apply for Medicaid at the time they wish to enter the nursing home. The government first calculates the family's assets and income. If these meet the qualifications, Medicaid then checks to see if the parents have made any gifts to their children or others within the last five years. If the parents have made any gifts that delay their qualification for Medicaid, the government uses a very simple formula. They are very thorough in checking all your parents' financial records, bank accounts, and investment reports. Let's assume your parents transferred $100,000 from their bank accounts to you four years ago, and your father has just entered a nursing home. The nursing home then applies for Medicaid to cover his costs.

The Feds then look over his records and determine that four years prior to entering the home, he gave you $100,000. They then divide this gift by the average monthly cost of a stay in the nursing home in your father's state to determine the number of months your dad is disqualified from getting Medicaid. In Massachusetts, that number was $7,380 in 2008. $100,000 divided by 7,380 is 13.5. That means Medicaid will not pay for his care for 13.5 months even though he qualifies based on current income and assets.

Gifts of all different kinds can disqualify you. Some families have tried some very subtle techniques to transfer assets from their parents to others. Setting up a joint account with a son or daughter and then removing the parent's name is one technique that is no longer allowed. Putting a home in the name of a son or daughter or other family member or friend fits into the same category. Purchasing a "life estate" in an adult child's home by paying off their mortgage is also disallowed.

A technique that often worked in the past was for your parents to transfer their assets to an insurance company for an immediate annuity to pay a monthly income. They planned that this would no longer count the lump sum as a countable asset. The state has

In the Tax Relief and Health Care Act of 2006, the government made it clear that they are eliminating all the loopholes that families can use to qualify their parents for Medicaid unless they are truly destitute.

countered that by comparing the amount of the annuity with the life expectancy of the recipient. If the projected payout exceeds their life expectancy, this difference will trigger a period of ineligibility. Even if the annuity is taken on the life of the healthy spouse, the state will require that the government be listed as the beneficiary of the annuity.

In the Tax Relief and Health Care Act of 2006, the government made it clear that they are eliminating all the loopholes that families can use to qualify their parents for Medicaid unless they are truly destitute. Medicaid has become a very large part of each state's budget, and they know that they must control its growth in the future.

Veterans Long-Term Care Benefits

The Department of Veterans Affairs (VA) provides three types of long-term care benefits for veterans. The first type is benefits provided to veterans enrolled in VA health care who have substantial service-connected disability. These medically necessary services include home care, hospice, respite care, assisted living, domiciliary care, geriatric assessments, and nursing home care.

Some of these services may be offered to veterans in the health care system who do not have service-connected disabilities but who may qualify because of low income or because they are receiving pension income from VA. These recipients may have to provide out-of-pocket copays or the services may only be available to these non-service-connected disabled veterans if the regional hospital has funds to cover them.

Currently, veterans desiring to join the health care system may be refused application because their income is too high or they do not qualify under other enrollment criteria. Increased demand in recent years for services and lack of congressional funding have forced VA to allow only certain classes of veterans to join the health care system.

The second type of benefit is state veterans homes. The U.S. Department of Veterans Affairs in conjunction with the states helps build and support state veterans homes. Money is provided by VA to help share the cost of construction with the state, and a subsidy of $71.42 a day is provided for each veteran using nursing home care in a state home. These facilities are generally available for any veteran and sometimes the non-veteran spouse. They are run by the states, often with the help of contract management. Most state veterans homes offer nursing home care but they may also offer assisted living, domiciliary care, and adult day care. There may be waiting lists for acceptance into veterans homes in some states.

State veterans homes are not free, but they are subsidized; however, the cost could be significantly less than a comparable facility in the private sector. Some of these homes can accept Medicaid payments. A complete list of state veterans homes can be found at http://www.longtermcarelink.net/ref_state_veterans_va_nursing_homes.htm

The third type of benefits for veterans is disability payments. These include compensation, pension, and survivor death benefits associated with compensation and death pension.

Compensation is designed to award the veteran a certain amount of monthly income to compensate for potential loss of income in the private sector due to a disability or injury or illness incurred in the service. In order to receive compensation, a veteran has to have evidence of a service-connected disability. Most veterans who are receiving this benefit were awarded an amount based on a percentage of disability when they left the service.

However, some veterans may have a military record of being exposed to extreme cold, having an in-service non-disabling injury, having tropical diseases, tuberculosis, or other incidents or exposures that may not have caused any disability at the time but years later have resulted in medical problems. In addition, some veterans may be receiving compensation but their condition has worsened and they may qualify for a higher disability rating. Veterans mentioned above may qualify for a first-time benefit or receive an increase in compensation amount. Applications should be made to see if they can receive an award. There is no income or asset test for compensation and the benefit is nontaxable.

Pension is available to all active duty veterans who served on active duty at least 90 days during a period of war. There is no need to have a service-connected disability to receive pension. To be eligible, the applicant must be totally disabled if he or she is younger than 65. Proof of disability is not required for applicants age 65 or over. Apparently, being old is evidence in itself of disability. Pension is sometimes known as the "aid and attendance benefit."

Veterans' service to qualify for pension would include World War II, the Korean Conflict, the Vietnam Conflict Period, and the Gulf War conflict. The veteran did not have to serve in combat but only had to be in the service during that period of time and only one day of the 90 days of service had to occur during the period of war.

Pension is available to all active duty veterans who served on active duty at least 90 days during a period of war.

The purpose of this benefit is to provide supplemental income to disabled or older veterans who have a low income. If the veteran's income exceeds the pension amount, there is no award.

Compensation and pension claims are submitted on the same form and VA will consider paying either benefit. For applications associated with the cost of home care, assisted living, or nursing home care, the pension benefit is a better option generally.

Pension can pay up to $1,843 a month to help offset the costs associated with home care, assisted living, nursing homes, and other un-reimbursed medical expenses. The amount of payment varies with the type of care, recipient income, and the marital status of the recipient. There are income and asset tests to qualify.

VA claims this benefit is only for low-income veterans. However, a special provision in the way the benefit is calculated for recurring medical expenses (long-term care costs associated with home care, assisted living, or nursing homes) could allow veteran households earning between $2,500 and $5,000 or more a month to qualify.

There are also death benefit payments associated with compensation and pension that are available to surviving spouses of veterans or surviving dependents.

The National Care Planning Council estimates that up to 33 percent of all Americans over the age of 65 might be eligible for a pension benefit under the right circumstances. That's how many war veterans or surviving spouses there are in this country. If your mother or father served in the armed forces, it is definitely worthwhile to check into the benefits that may be available to them.

Is Long-Term Care Insurance Necessary?

So where does all this leave your parents in preparing for a catastrophic illness? Unless their financial resources are extremely limited already, they have three choices:

- Use their investment and retirement assets to pay for care.

- Tap into their home equity using a reverse mortgage or a home equity loan.

- Buy long-term care insurance.

In the past, many advisors and financial authorities were very cynical about long-term care insurance, but that has changed dramatically in the last 10 years. Long-term care insurance has improved significantly in that period of time. Companies have improved benefits and expanded coverage to provide care at home, adult day care, and assisted-living facilities, as well as nursing homes.

In the past, many advisors and financial authorities were very cynical about long-term care insurance, but that has changed dramatically in the last 10 years. Long-term care insurance has improved significantly in that period of time.

As a matter of fact, most long-term care insurance claims are paid to people who are at home. In the past, the average age that most people bought coverage was in their sixties. But now because of their experience with their parents, many younger people are buying coverage. The average age of a purchaser will soon be in the fifties. People buy coverage at younger ages for two reasons. First, the annual premium costs are lower. The younger you are, the lower the annual cost. Once you have established the premium based on your age, the insurance company cannot increase your premium without increasing everyone's premium in your state who falls in the same category with the same policy. In addition, each state can deny an insurance company's application to increase rates for its residents.

Second, many people buy coverage at a younger age because they want to buy it when they are healthy and assured of qualifying for coverage. If you have certain health impairments, you may no longer be able to buy coverage. I recently had a client who, at age 56, had elected to delay buying long-term care coverage. She just felt she wasn't ready to make a decision. Six months later, she called me and said she was ready to apply for coverage. I sent her an application, but two weeks later received an e-mail from her. She told me that she had just been diagnosed with multiple sclerosis. Now she will never be able to buy coverage, and she will certainly need it.

With the Deficit Reduction Act of 2005, President Bush made it possible for all states to participate in a Partnership for Long-term Care (PLTC) with insurance companies. Previous to this act, partnerships had only been set up in four states: Connecticut, New York, Indiana, and California. The partnership allows Medicaid to work together with insurance companies to protect a family's assets. If an insurance plan is approved by the state as a partnership program, the amount of insurance coverage that an individual uses up for their care allows them to protect the same amount of assets and still qualify for Medicaid.

For example, let's say that your father has a long-term care insurance plan providing $200 a day for three years. That's a total of $219,000 of coverage. Let's also assume that the insurance company has paid out that amount for your father's care. Now, if he continues to need care, you will have to use up his assets to pay for it. Under the partnership program, since his insurance policy was approved by the state, he will be allowed to protect up to $219,000 of countable assets and still qualify for Medicaid. Normally he would have to use up most of this $219,000 to qualify for Medicaid. However, the partnership program allows him to retain the assets and still qualify for Medicaid assistance. This provides a significant advantage for many individuals to protect a portion of their assets for their families.

Companies have improved benefits and expanded coverage to provide care at home, adult day care, and assisted-living facilities, as well as nursing homes.

Why are some states offering this partnership program? They have determined that it will eventually cost them less in total Medicaid expenses if they offer state residents an incentive to purchase long-term care. The insurance company takes on the initial risk of paying for care, reducing the ultimate number of people who may qualify for Medicaid, and the resulting costs to the state.

In addition, the IRS has provided additional tax incentives for individuals to own long-term care insurance. If any individual receives a long-term care benefit from an insurance company, it will not be considered taxable income. If the benefit is greater than $260 a day, it will be considered tax-free if the full amount is used for care. Policyholders can also deduct a portion of their premiums as a medical expense based on their age (see Table 1). Medical expenses in excess of 7.5 percent of adjusted gross income are tax-deductible, and the premium allowed would count toward that number.

Table 1. Tax-Deductible Long-Term Care Insurance Premiums in 2008. *The tax deduction on your tax return for a qualified long-term care insurance policy's premium is limited.*

AGE	MAXIMUM TAX-DEDUCTIBLE PREMIUM
Under 41	$280
41-50	$530
51-60	$1,060
61-70	$2,830
Over 70	$3,530

The IRS has also made it attractive for businesses to provide long-term care insurance coverage to their key people. In the traditional corporation, a business owner can select key people (including him or herself) and have the business pay for the long-term care for those employees and their spouses without it being considered taxable income to that person. In addition, the business can deduct what it spends on the premium. Finally, if any employee or spouse receives benefits from the policy, the money received is not taxable. The government has made long-term care a benefit with significant tax advantages for the employer and employee.

The IRS has also made it attractive for businesses to provide long-term care insurance coverage to their key people.

Insurance companies have increased the types of care that will be covered under a long-term care plan. It is no longer considered just nursing home insurance. Most good plans cover home care, assisted-living care, adult day care, hospice care, homemaker services, and respite care. Respite care is offered to allow a caregiver spouse to take a break from providing care to his or her spouse. A *care coordinator* is provided to help the family put together a care plan for the best and most appropriate services. In many cases, families can select their own care provider for home services rather than use a health care agency. The only restriction is that the paid caregiver cannot be a family member.

To qualify for insurance coverage under most long-term care policies, a doctor must certify that the person is unable to do two or more of the activities of daily living. These activities include bathing, toileting, eating, transferring in and out of bed, dressing, and walking. In addition, cognitive impairment from dementia or Alzheimer's is covered. Plans are either reimbursement or indemnity plans. Reimbursement plans reimburse the insured for those expenses incurred in their care. Indemnity plans pay a full daily benefit once you qualify for as long as you need care without the necessity to prove expenses incurred. Indemnity plans are more expensive than reimbursement plans.

Which Long-Term Care Policy is Best?

The cost of a long-term care policy is based on a number of factors. When you purchase a plan, you select the maximum daily benefit the insurance company will pay. This usually varies from $50 to $400 per day. You select a waiting period ranging from 20 days to 180 days or more. This is like a deductible. It is the period of time you must self-insure.

Then you select a benefit period. This is the period of time coverage will continue once you begin receiving care. It can range from two years to an unlimited period. Most plans provide an adjustment to the benefit paid for inflation — a *cost-of-living rider*. With this rider, coverage per day increases each year by a compounded 5 percent. This benefit is especially important for a person who buys coverage when they are relatively young.

In selecting a long-term care policy, it is very important to look at the financial stability of the insurance company providing the coverage. How long have they been in the business? How much have they paid out in claims? How many policyholders do they have? If you or your parents are intending to need this benefit five or ten years or more from now, you want to make sure that the company is financially sound.

In selecting a long-term care policy, it is very important to look at the financial stability of the insurance company providing the coverage.

Long-term care insurance is relatively expensive compared to other forms of insurance. But the actual cost of long-term care can be very high and devastating to a family. In many states, the cost of care is more than $7,000 per month. Are you willing to risk your parent's assets under those circumstances? How long would your parents assets last if either one of them needed care for two or three years or more? As a family, you must evaluate this risk. If your parents cannot afford to pay the premiums with their own resources, it might be well worth it for the adult children to help supplement the cost or take full responsibility to pay the insurance company.

Your parents may be opposed to paying the costs of long-term care insurance because, like auto insurance, if they don't use it, the premium goes to the insurance company with no benefit back to them. As a result of this concern, the industry has developed several hybrid products that provide long-term care insurance as well as other permanent benefits. One of these is a life insurance policy that incorporates long-term care insurance within it. This type of policy can be purchased with a one-time payment or, in some cases, an annual premium like traditional life insurance.

One of my clients told me he was not interested in paying long-term care premiums that he would never recover if he didn't need the care. He purchased a life insurance policy with a single payment of $100,000. He immediately had $165,000 of life insurance if he died. At the same time, he was able to choose a long-term care benefit equal to 2 percent of the death benefit for four years as part of the policy. This meant that his life insurance policy would pay up to $3,300 per month for long-term care for four years. If he did not use the long-term care benefit, the life insurance benefit would be paid out to his beneficiary at his death. If he did use the long-term care benefit, the life insurance death benefit would be reduced to a minimum guaranteed amount. In this way, he felt he was getting the full value for his premium dollars.

If your parents have life insurance policies that they have had for a long time and the death benefit is not critical to them because they have other assets, they can actually sell that policy.

In addition to life insurance policies, some annuities have long-term care benefits. These annuities pay out a guaranteed rate of interest and build up a cash fund that can be used to pay for long-term care. As long as the interest is deferred in the annuity, you do not pay taxes on the gain. The gain is only taxed (as ordinary income) when you make withdrawals from the contract. If the cash value of the annuity is not used to pay for long-term care, your parents can pass the annuity on to their heirs. They designate a beneficiary in the contract. Unlike life insurance, however, the beneficiary must pay taxes on the gain when they receive it. Life insurance benefits are received tax-free.

If your parents have life insurance policies that they have had for a long time and the death benefit is not critical to them because they have other assets, they can actually sell that policy. This is called a "life settlement." This is available to older people who are not ill. They can sell a life insurance policy to a life settlement company for a specific amount. This amount is based on a formula, which includes the policy's cash value, the benefit to be paid at death, and the age of the insured. Your parents can use the proceeds of the sale of the policy to pay for long-term care needs. But they should carefully evaluate whether or not to sell a life insurance policy they have had for a long time. The actual cost of the insurance might be quite low, and when the death benefit is paid out, the beneficiaries will receive it tax-free. In addition, they may feel very uncomfortable knowing that some stranger owns a life insurance policy on their life.

The Bottom Line

There are many factors to consider and plan for when you evaluate the risk of your parents needing extensive health care. You need to plan now for that possibility because you never know what extent and type of care will be needed. The onset of an acute or chronic illness can be sudden and unpredictable. Planning for the unknown can be difficult and unsettling, but it is well worth the effort.

Chapter 8
Leaving a Legacy

Have you talked with your parents to determine if they want to leave something behind after they're gone — some symbol of what they believe in or have fought for during their lives? In other words, do they want to leave a legacy? Is there some organization or cause that has been meaningful to them? Do they want to be remembered by the members of their church or synagogue or some other group?

Take the time to talk with your parents about leaving a legacy. Perhaps this conversation will occur at a family meeting or in a more casual setting. You need to ask them a specific, sometimes difficult question, such as, "Mom, Dad, how do you want to be remembered after you're gone?" Ask the question, and them sit back and listen.

What is Your Parents' Legacy?

It's possible that they want to be remembered by their family for being good and loving parents, but it's also possible that they want to have an impact on organizations that they have been a part of or causes that they believe in deeply. You won't know the answer until you ask, but asking any questions about your parents' mortality is difficult. These kinds of questions are often taboo between parents and their adult children. You just may find out, however, that they have been waiting for someone to pose this question and might have a lot to say.

"Mom, Dad, how do you want to be remembered after you're gone?" Ask the question, and then sit back and listen.

Certainly your parents should tell you that they want you to remember beliefs or traditions. These can be communicated at the family meeting or in a letter attached to their wills. What family traditions do they want to be maintained? Is it a special family gathering in the summer or a Thanksgiving dinner with all the members of Dad's side of the family in attendance? Perhaps it might be a special wish related to their religious beliefs. It is important to give them a vehicle to communicate these wishes. Create an opportunity for them to make these family wishes known.

Helping a Charity

In addition to wishes for their family, your parents may want to recognize their church, synagogue, or another organization. There are a number of ways to do this that not only benefit the organization but benefit your parents as well. The simplest thing to do is to name the organization in their wills. This is known as a bequest. Your parents can state that a specific amount of money or a percentage of their estate goes to the organization. It can be made as a restricted gift for a specific purpose such as buying a new organ or benefiting the church school. It can also be an unrestricted gift allowing the organization to use the funds for whatever purpose they find necessary.

In addition to wishes for their family, your parents may want to recognize their church, synagogue, or another organization. There are a number of ways to do this that not only benefit the organization, but benefit your parents as well.

Another very simple way to make a contribution to a charity or church is through life insurance. If your parents own a life insurance policy, they can name a charity as one of the beneficiaries. For example, if your father has a $100,000 life insurance policy and he no longer needs the full amount of coverage because he has built up his other assets, he can request a change of beneficiary form. With this form, he can split the primary beneficiaries between your mother and a charity. He can specify the amount going to the organization or a percentage of the death benefit.

The funds donated to the organization reduce your insured parent's taxable estate and potential income or estate tax. There are also other methods that your parents can use to benefit from the gift while they are alive. One of these is called a *charitable remainder trust* (CRT). This is an arrangement in which property or money is donated to the charity, but the donor continues to receive income from it while they are alive. By donating property such as stock or real estate that appreciates significantly in value, your parents can avoid paying capital gains tax on the gift.

One type of charitable remainder trust is called a *charitable remainder unitrust* (CRUT). The CRUT is designed to pay an annual income to one or more persons (the beneficiaries) for a set period or for their lifetime. When the individuals give property or cash to a charity, the amount of income they receive is based on the value of the assets in the trust multiplied by a percentage rate that is determined when the trust is created. When they set up the trust, the donor receives a current tax deduction that is calculated based on a number of factors that includes:

- The type of charity
- The type of property donated
- The payout percentage elected at the creation of the trust
- The term of years that income is to be paid to the beneficiaries

There are other variations of the CRT. One is called the *charitable remainder annuity trust* (CRAT). Like the CRUT, the individual makes a gift of property, stock, cash, or some other form of capital to a charity. The charity then sells the property, invests the proceeds, and pays an income to the beneficiaries based on the terms of the trust. With the CRAT, the income amount stays the same each year no matter how much the principal changes. The CRUT income can vary because it is based on a specific percentage of the capital remaining in the trust each year.

One of my clients worked for a large corporation most of his life. He bought some of the company stock every year he worked there. By the time he was in his sixties, he had accumulated a large amount of the company stock. If he sold it, he would have had to pay a large capital gain. At approximately the same time he was planning to attend the 50th reunion of his college class. As a gift to the college, he placed a large portion of the stock in a charitable remainder trust that the college offered. As a result, he was acknowledged for making a significant gift. The college then sold the stock in the trust and invested it to produce income for my client. He began receiving a very attractive income from the charitable trust and, in the future when he dies, the college will receive the principal. By making the gift, his income was significantly greater than if he sold this stock and invested it in an income-producing investment. In addition, he removed the stock and its growth from his estate for tax purposes. My client chose the type of charitable remainder trust known as a CRAT. He will receive a specific set amount of income each month for the rest of his life. This income must be a least 5 percent of the principal.

If you, as a son or daughter of a parent who has set up a charitable remainder trust, are concerned that they are giving away assets that could be passed on to you or your children, you might suggest that they use a *wealth replacement trust*. With a portion of the amount they get from the charitable remainder trust each year, they buy life insurance that replaces the amount given. At their death, the life insurance proceeds are paid into a wealth replacement trust. The proceeds are then paid out to the beneficiaries of the trust based on your parents' wishes. This technique works well if at least one of your parents is healthy enough to qualify for a life insurance policy.

In some cases, your parents may want to make a gift to their favorite institutions over a period of time. But they might want to get the tax deduction for the gift this year. Through a very simple vehicle known as a *donor-advised fund*, they can give a significant amount to a special fund and dole out gifts from it each year as they see fit. When they make the initial gift, they get the tax deduction, and each year they are required to transfer at least 5 percent of the fund to IRS-approved charities. Many mutual fund companies offer these funds at a very reasonable cost. For approximately 1 percent per year, they will send out all the checks to the organizations you name and keep a record of each for you. The funds can be invested in a number of different ways including various types of stocks and bonds.

An extension of the donor-advised fund is a *private foundation*. It acts like a donor-advised fund but is much larger in scope. Donors who establish a private foundation expect to transfer a very large amount of money to it. Bill Gates is probably the best-known individual who has established a private foundation. He and his wife, Melinda, gave over $31 billion to establish the Bill and Melinda Gates Foundation. Their goal has been to improve health care throughout the world through their foundation.

Tax Laws and Charitable Giving

At age 70½, your parents are required to take money out of their individual retirement accounts each year. This is called the required minimum distribution; the amount they must take out is based on their life expectancy. One of three methods is used by the IRS to determine how much must be taken out.

If your mother and father's ages are less than 10 years apart, the IRS requires that they use the Uniform Lifetime Table to determine how much must be taken out of their IRAs. For example, if your father is 71 and your mother is 68, the table states that their joint life expectancy is 26.5 years. To determine how much your father must take out of his IRA, take the value of his IRA on December 31 of the previous year and divide that number by 26.5 . Let's assume the value was $100,000 on December 31, 2006. His required distribution for 2007 would be $100,000 divided by 26.5, or $3,773.58. Each year, the required minimum increases as your parents get older.

This required minimum must be taken each year based on the total value of your parents' IRAs if they are over 70½. You must add together the value of all their IRAs and divide that total by the required number from the chart. But let's assume that your parents don't need the full amount of those distributions each year. They might designate one of their IRAs as their charity IRA. Your dad has to take a distribution from it anyway. He would have to pay tax on that distribution as he took it each year. What if he turned around and gave that distribution to his church? He would then get a tax deduction for the gift, offsetting the tax he has to pay on the distribution.

All of these techniques are based on your parents' interest in leaving something behind to the organizations that have meant a lot to them. The number of charities they select is based on their generosity and their ability to give. You, as their adult child, must recognize their desire to leave a legacy and help them to do so. Your parents have spent a lifetime accumulating the money that they have. It is their decision as to where that money should go and who should benefit from it. Your role is to help them accomplish their goals in the simplest and most effective way.

The Bottom Line

Don't forget to ask your parents the important question, "How do you want to be remembered after you're gone?" Listen to their wishes, and help them come up with a solution that will benefit charities for years to come while taking care of their own financial needs.

Chapter 9
Special Situations

When we think of our parents getting older, we assume that Mom and Dad will live into their seventies or eighties, and that Dad will pass away first and leave everything to Mom. When Mom dies in her eighties, everything will go to her children. But in an age when older people are living longer, this is not always the case.

Second Marriages

One of my clients, a recently retired doctor, was in his seventies when he discovered that his wife had cancer. She became increasingly sick and incapacitated. Fortunately, one of her best friends who was a widow lived with them and took care of the dying wife in her last days. During the months spent taking care of the doctor's sick wife, the friend became very close to the doctor. Surprisingly, within a year after the doctor's wife passed away, he married her best friend and caretaker.

Early in the marriage, the new wife confided in me that her greatest fear was that if her new husband died, his children would demand that the home was theirs and force her to leave. She could have protected herself if she had asked him to redraft a will and name her to inherit his home. If he had done this, however, he would have eventually passed the house to her children, not his own. At her death, the house would then go to her children.

A better option for his children would be to give his new wife the life use of the property and then pass it on to his children at her death. They would still eventually get the property, but they would have to wait until she passed away. She wasn't comfortable with this option and pressed him to build a new home for the two of them. I wasn't really surprised when about a year after they married, the doctor called me and told me that they were going to sell their current home and build a new one. It was clear that his new wife had taken control to protect herself. The new home was based on her design and ideas, and the doctor spent a great deal of his wealth having it built and decorated.

In another situation, another client of mine retired after a long career as a very well-known family physician. Unfortunately, shortly after he retired, he learned that his wife had Alzheimer's. The first few years of his retirement were occupied with taking care of her and finally putting her into a nursing home. Within months, she no longer knew who he was. In his despair, he contacted the widow of another doctor who had been a long-time friend. They started seeing each other often, and their meetings turned into a romantic relationship. Shortly after his first wife died, he married the widow of his close friend.

Although his new wife lived a very luxurious lifestyle and had a very strong balance sheet, she didn't have a great deal of cash or at least didn't want to spend it. I noticed my client taking increasingly larger withdrawals from his retirement plan. After several months of watching this pattern, I called him in to discuss the situation. He informed me that he was loaning the money to his new wife to completely renovate her very large old house and to purchase a condo in Florida. Unfortunately, every withdrawal he took from his IRA to help her pay expenses was taxable as income to him.

Since he has remarried, I have watched his retirement plan get smaller and smaller. Recently, I made it clear to him that he probably would run out of money within the next two years. At age 76, he will have to depend entirely on his new wife for income the rest of his life. He seemed powerless to do anything about the situation. I informed him that the worst possible situation might be if his wife predeceased him and her children expected their inheritance. He would be left destitute.

If the judge rules that the parent is incompetent, he or she will name a conservator. The conservator must be of good character and capable of effectively managing the parent's affairs.

Protecting Your Parents in Second Marriages

Unfortunately, in neither of these situations were the children of my clients aware of what was happening to their fathers' assets. Unless I observed some inability of the client to act or think rationally, I had no right to inform the adult children. These individuals were my clients and I was required to keep their financial affairs confidential. But what could the children do if they saw their parent entering into a situation with a new wife or husband who was quickly going through their assets?

The first step would be for the children to have a meeting with their parent to discuss the situation. This is often very difficult because it puts the children in a position of appearing to be the money-hungry heirs even if they are acting in their parent's best interest. Most likely their parent will defend his actions as merely trying to take care of his spouse. In the end, he has the right to spend his money any way he wants without answering to his children.

The second and more difficult step is for the children to have their parent declared incompetent, become his conservator, and have the authority to manage his financial affairs. This is a difficult and time-consuming process. A parent may be declared incompetent if he or she is no longer able to manage his or her financial affairs. Generally, the parent's attending physician must certify this. A hearing is set in probate court and conducted by a probate judge. The attending physician will have to testify that the parent is not capable of making financial decisions. An attorney can represent the parent.

If the judge rules that the parent is incompetent, he or she will name a conservator. The conservator must be of good character and capable of effectively managing the parent's affairs. The judge could name a healthy spouse or one of the parent's adult children as conservator. Once the adult child or spouse is named conservator, he or she must file an annual accounting with the probate court. This accounting lists every transaction that the conservator conducted with the parent's money. In most cases, the conservator hires an accountant and a lawyer to complete this report.

The way to avoid this uncomfortable situation in the first place is for you to encourage your parents to do some planning in advance. It would be best for them to meet with the attorney who drafted their wills and trusts and discuss what happens to their assets when either one of them dies or the other spouse remarries. This may be a very difficult conversation, but it is valuable to do it while they are both alive and thinking clearly. Often an attorney will suggest having a certain portion of your parent's assets going into a trust. A separate trustee is named (someone other than your surviving parent) to oversee the assets. The surviving parent has access to the income from the trust and limited access to the principal. At the death of the second parent, the assets then go to the children or grandchildren.

By setting up this trust, you avoid the possibility of a spouse from a second marriage diverting all the family assets to themselves or their children from your surviving mom or dad.

Special-Needs Siblings

Another special situation involves your parents and a brother or sister of yours who has special needs. This may be a child who had a serious accident and suffered permanent injury or a child suffering from serious mental illness. In any case, your parents are concerned that when they die there will be no one left to care for the child or who has the assets to make sure that the child is taken care of. Again, your parents should consult with an estate planning attorney to set up a *special needs trust* — sometimes called a *supplemental needs trust*. This is a very unique trust designed to protect an individual who has a disability.

A special needs or supplemental needs trust enables a person with a physical or mental disability or a chronic illness to have an unlimited amount of assets held in trust for his or her benefit. If the trust is drafted properly, these assets are not counted for disqualification from Medicaid. In other words, the individual can still qualify for Medicaid payments or Social Security disability payments and have a significant amount of assets within this trust.

Normally, a person must be impoverished to qualify for Medicaid; however, it is usually the case that these assets revert to the government to reimburse them for Medicaid payments if the individual should die.

One of my clients has an adult child who had a motorcycle accident and suffered a serious brain injury. The son now lives at home with his parents who are retired. They have two other children; however, one of these children is a daughter who is single mother with two young children. The other is a son who has settled about 3,000 miles away with his own family. As a result, my clients don't believe that either of these children could be expected to take care of their brother. They have set up a special needs trust for that child which will be funded primarily with life insurance. My clients purchased a special type of life insurance known as a *second-to-die policy*. When the second spouse dies, the life insurance proceeds will be paid into the trust. These funds will then be used for the care of the disabled child.

A special needs or supplemental needs trust enables a person with a physical or mental disability or a chronic illness to have held in trust for his or her benefit an unlimited amount of assets.

Irresponsible Siblings

There are other situations where your parents may want to protect their assets from the next generation. One of your siblings might have a spouse who is a notorious big spender and completely irresponsible with money, or one of your brothers or sisters might have a serious drug, gambling, or alcohol problem. In each of these situations, your parents might be reluctant to leave the child with a large amount of money which they might spend irresponsibly.

In their book, *Beyond the Grave*, Gerald and Jeffrey Condon describe an excellent way to protect the inheritance of one of your siblings that might have an addiction, a credit problem, marital problems, or other financial difficulties. It is called a *protection trust* When your parents die, their money and property does not go directly to the difficult child. It goes to the trustee of the Protection Trust. The trustee manages all the assets that go into this trust, which may include real estate, stocks, bonds, cash, and even jewelry.

The trustee also makes decisions regarding the distribution of income or any principal to the child. He makes these decisions based on the instructions made by your parents in the trust before they died. The amount of protection built into the trust is based on your parents' desire to control the spending of their money by that child after they are gone. One of the child's brothers or sisters could be named as the trustee. It might be better to name a trusted advisor or possibly an institution as trustee. It could be very difficult for another family member to act as trustee, especially if the child puts a lot of pressure on them to have access to the money.

One of my clients had named his daughter to be one of the trustees of his estate. She previously had difficulties managing an alcohol problem when she was younger, but had gotten married, had children, and seemed to be getting her life on track. One day my client called me, clearly distressed, and told me that his daughter had disappeared. One night when her husband came home, she said she had to go out and pick something up at the store. She didn't return from the store and was actually missing for several weeks. She had gone on an alcohol binge. My client asked that she be removed as a trustee of his assets and that a protection trust be set up for her. The trust would provide an income for her, but stipulated that if she had another relapse or could not control herself, the money would be cut off.

The Bottom Line

Dealing with all the family issues that may arise can be very challenging. Your parents will never have all the answers they need to do everything perfectly when they pass on their assets to their children. All you can do is help them to make the right decisions for their family. They may choose to ignore family difficulties or they may become quite involved in setting things up properly. The bottom line is that it is their money and they will make the final decisions on how it is handled.

Chapter 10
Organizing Your Parents' Important Information (The Lifefolio)

D ealing with your parent's death will likely be a stressful and emotionally draining experience. In a very short period of time, you will have to make a number of difficult decisions. Prepare yourself as best you can for this traumatic event by gathering together all the necessary information in advance.

I have labeled the section that follows this one the "Lifefolio." It contains the forms you will need to complete to get a handle on your parents' affairs. I have included a checklist which will help you complete those actions you need to take when they die. There are sections that require your parents' input, including their values and the possessions that they consider emotionally important, as well as their educational and occupational background. Leave these forms with your parents for awhile. Let them have some time to think about them.

Dealing with your parent's death will likely be a stressful and emotionally draining experience.

Funeral Planning

Your parents should make decisions regarding their funeral planning in advance when there is time to reflect. They will need to communicate with you if they wish to donate their organs, if they wish to be cremated, and what they want done with their remains. They may have some specific thoughts about the type of funeral service they want, who they want there, and what type of music they want played.

In many cases, the funeral home your parents select will be able to write their obituaries, but you might want to attempt this yourself. Review some obituaries that are in the paper. Gather some important facts about your parents. Their obituaries do not have to be long, but you want to capture something unique about them as well as summarize the landmark events in their life. I suggest you write the obituary while your parent is still alive. Once he or she has passed away, you will have a number of things to do and a very short period of time in which to do them. You will probably be emotionally strained and perhaps not thinking quite clearly. It is best to write the obituary when you can reflect and have the time to do a good job.

Are you going to give the eulogy at the funeral service? What do you want to say? I have found that the eulogies that are most moving not only include some serious and important facts about the deceased but some lighter, more humorous anecdotes that define his or her personality. Presenting a eulogy can be very difficult for you emotionally, but it can be a very satisfying experience. It gives you the opportunity to share what you loved about your mom or dad with your friends and family. It is also a form of completion, a way to say goodbye to them.

Executor Duties

If you are named the executor of your parent's estate, you will be required to do a number of things to settle the estate. First, of course, you will be required to find the most current copy of their will. You will find the executor named there. If your parents have trusts, the

It is important that you, as executor, keep accurate records of all income and expenses of your parent's estate.

trustees will be named. You must notify the trustees as soon as possible. At this point, it is a good idea to identify an attorney who is experienced in settling estates to help you. The attorney should provide you with legal and practical advice to get through the estate settlement process. Before you get too far, find out how much the attorney charges. Some attorneys work strictly on an hourly rate; others request a percentage of the estate to settle it.

Next, you need to get many original copies of the death certificate to provide to insurance companies, brokerage firms, and other holders of assets in your parent's name. You will then need to do an inventory of all your parent's assets. If your parent owns real estate, it is possible that certified appraisal of the property would be required. You must determine the value of all assets on the date of death. With stocks, that means the average cost of the stock on the day of your parent's death. The attorney and the probate court will most likely review this inventory.

You must then establish a brokerage account at an investment firm in the name of your parent's estate to hold all stocks, bonds, and mutual funds. As executor, you will be the only one with authority to make any changes to this portfolio. Only investments that are in that parent's name will go into this account. Any investments that are jointly held with your other parent will be changed to that parent's name alone. If there is a trust, the trustee will set up a trust account to hold all assets in the trust.

It is important that you, as executor, keep accurate records of all income and expenses of your parent's estate. Set up an estate checking account. It is very important not to mix any of your personal assets with the assets of your parent's estate. As the executor, it is your responsibility to pay all your parent's bills and settle any debts that he or she might have. Pay them from the estate checking account that you have set up. You will also need to inform all beneficiaries on a regular basis of the status of any estate assets and life insurance policies. It is important to give them a projected date when the assets will be distributed.

Assets, Insurance, and Taxes

You must find all life insurance policies and annuities and notify the insurance companies that your parent is deceased. The proceeds of life insurance policies will normally be paid into a special money market account set up at the insurance company in the name of the beneficiary. If the primary beneficiary is deceased, the proceeds will go to the contingent beneficiaries according to the percentages that your parent established when they set up the policy. If there are no contingent beneficiaries, then life insurance assets will go to the estate through the probate process. Life insurance proceeds will be received income tax free by the beneficiaries.

If your parent had an annuity, the rules are different than for life insurance policies. Your parent names a beneficiary like a life insurance policy, but the proceeds are taxed differently. As I mentioned previously, the beneficiary receives life insurance proceeds tax-free. The gain in an annuity is taxed as ordinary income like wages or salaries. If one of your parents names the other as beneficiary of an annuity, the surviving parent can keep the annuity without having to pay tax during his or her lifetime.

If the beneficiary is not a surviving spouse, the beneficiary has to choose how to receive the annuity assets. In the first 12 months following the death of the annuity holder (*annuitant*), the beneficiary can choose to receive an income spread out over any period as long as his or her lifetime. However, if the beneficiary doesn't make a decision in the first 12 months after the annuitant dies, the only choice is to receive the funds within a five-year period. In both cases, the portion of the money received as earnings (not principal) is taxed as income.

If your parent had an IRA or other retirement account, the rules are similar to an annuity. If he or she names their surviving spouse as beneficiary, the spouse can roll the assets over into his or her own account without paying taxes. If the spouse is no longer alive, the beneficiaries will be required to set up an *inherited IRA*. They cannot mix this IRA with their other IRA assets. They have the choice of taking the proceeds out of the IRA on a schedule based on their single life expectancy provided by the IRS or sooner if they choose to do so. Everything they withdraw is taxable as income.

As executor, you must be aware of the income tax and estate tax implications of anything that you do in settling the estate. The advice of your financial advisor, estate attorney, or accountant is very important. The tax basis for any assets received by beneficiaries is the value at the time of your parent's death. In other words, if they owned a stock and paid $10 a share for it, if the value at their death was $100 a share, the new basis for the beneficiary is $100 a share. This means all the gain is forgiven for tax purposes. If the beneficiary then sells the stock, his or her tax is based on the gain or loss above or below the $100 inherited value.

Succession Tax

Based on the size of your parents' estates, if you are executor, you may be required to pay state or federal estate taxes for them. The succession tax varies from state to state. The amount taxed according to federal estate tax law is changing each year up until 2010. If a person dies in 2008 with an estate of $2 million, the executor will have to pay estate tax at a rate of 45 percent on the assets over that level. If a person dies in 2009, the limit is increased to $3.5 million. If a person dies in 2010, there is no federal estate tax, and if a person dies in 2011 or later, the rule reverts back to the old law with estates of over $1 million taxed at a rate of 55 percent.

It is very likely that Congress will change the estate tax law before it reverts to the old schedule. If you are an executor, you must file federal and state tax returns for your parent's estate during the settlement period. The most difficult of these is the IRS Form 706 — the United States Estate (and Generation-Skipping Transfer) Tax Return. You must include the value of all estate assets at death, any gifts that have been made, and any estate deductions on this form. I would advise you to have an accountant or attorney help you complete this.

The Bottom Line

Please assist your parents in completing as many of the Lifefolio forms as possible. The more information you gather now, the easier it will be to prepare their estates. I am sure that your parents will also have peace of mind knowing that their affairs are recorded and in good order.

Lifefolio

Guide for Survivors

What to Do at the Time of Death

- ❏ Immediately authorize donation of body parts (authorize organ donation prior to death) if applicable.
- ❏ Contact medical school for body bequeathal if applicable.
- ❏ Contact funeral director or memorial society.
- ❏ Notify friends, relatives, and employer.
- ❏ Maintain a list of flowers, cards, donations, and other expressions of sympathy.
- ❏ Arrange for friends and relatives to help as needed (childcare, shopping, cooking, telephones, etc.)
- ❏ Arrange for funeral or memorial service.
- ❏ Arrange for cemetery lot, mausoleum, or crypt if applicable.
- ❏ Submit obituary information to newspaper.
- ❏ Arrange for after-service luncheon or gathering for friends and relatives.
- ❏ Obtain a minimum of eight certified copies of death certificates.

What to Do after the Funeral or Memorial Service

- ❏ Send notes to acknowledge expressions of sympathy.
- ❏ Notify life insurance companies and file claim forms.
- ❏ Notify other insurance providers and file claims where applicable.
    - ❏ Medical, health, disability, accident and travel
    - ❏ Vehicle
    - ❏ Residence
- ❏ Apply for appropriate benefits.
    - ❏ Social Security benefits
    - ❏ Veteran's burial benefits and other applicable benefits
    - ❏ Pension benefits
    - ❏ Workers' compensation benefits
- ❏ Meet with lawyer to commence probate proceedings if needed.
    - ❏ Take original will and copies of forms in this book.
    - ❏ Assist with inventory of assets, etc.
- ❏ Notify accountant/tax preparer (unless estate lawyer is preparing final tax returns).
    - ❏ Take copies of appropriate forms in this book.
    - ❏ Take copies of recent tax returns.
- ❏ Notify investment advisors.
    - ❏ Change ownership of joint stocks by removing name of decedent.
    - ❏ Suspend any open orders of the decedent.
    - ❏ Set up estate account for decedent.
- ❏ Notify banker(s).
    - ❏ Change ownership of joint accounts by removing name of decedent.
- ❏ Notify credit card companies.
    - ❏ Close accounts and destroy cards. In some cases, an authorized signer may apply to take over account in his or her name.
- ❏ Contact airlines to apply to transfer frequent flyer miles to primary beneficiary unless otherwise assigned in will.

People to Contact

Professional Advisors

My lawyer is _____
Address _____
City_____ State _____ Zip _____
E-mail_____ Phone_____

My accountant/tax preparer is _____
Address _____
City_____ State _____ Zip _____
E-mail_____ Phone_____

My dentist is _____
Address _____
City_____ State _____ Zip _____
E-mail_____ Phone_____

My financial advisor is _____
Address _____
City_____ State _____ Zip _____
E-mail_____ Phone_____

My personal physician is _____
Address _____
City_____ State _____ Zip _____
E-mail_____ Phone_____

My specialty physician is _____
Address _____
City_____ State _____ Zip _____
E-mail_____ Phone_____

My specialty physician is _____
Address _____
City_____ State _____ Zip _____
E-mail_____ Phone_____

My _____ is _____
Address _____
City_____ State _____ Zip _____
E-mail_____ Phone_____

Service Providers for My Child(ren) and Home

My _____ is _____

Address _____

City_____ State _____ Zip _____

E-mail_____ Phone _____

My child(ren)'s legal guardian is _____

Address _____

City_____ State _____ Zip _____

E-mail_____ Phone _____

My child(ren)'s school or day care provider is _____

Address _____

City_____ State _____ Zip _____

E-mail_____ Phone _____

My child(ren)'s other school or day care provider is _____

Address _____

City_____ State _____ Zip _____

E-mail_____ Phone _____

My child(ren)'s babysitter is _____

Address _____

City_____ State _____ Zip _____

E-mail_____ Phone _____

My child(ren)'s physician provider is _____

Address _____

City_____ State _____ Zip _____

E-mail_____ Phone _____

My child(ren)'s dentist is _____

Address _____

City_____ State _____ Zip _____

E-mail_____ Phone _____

My child(ren)'s _____ is _____

Address _____

City_____ State _____ Zip _____

E-mail_____ Phone _____

Service Providers for My Child(ren) and Home (continued)

List other service providers to contact such as house cleaning service, gardener, pool maintenance service, or rental property management company.

Service provider _____

Type of service _____

Address _____

City_____ State _____ Zip _____

E-mail_____ Phone_____

Service provider _____

Type of service _____

Address _____

City_____ State _____ Zip _____

E-mail_____ Phone_____

Service provider _____

Type of service _____

Address _____

City_____ State _____ Zip _____

E-mail_____ Phone_____

Service provider _____

Type of service _____

Address _____

City_____ State _____ Zip _____

E-mail_____ Phone_____

Service provider _____

Type of service _____

Address _____

City_____ State _____ Zip _____

E-mail_____ Phone_____

Service provider _____

Type of service _____

Address _____

City_____ State _____ Zip _____

E-mail_____ Phone_____

Where to Find Records and Keys

Keep original documents that are valuable or irreplaceable in a safe-deposit box. Keep copies of originals in your home filing system.

Personal History

Safe-Deposit Box   **Other Locations**

- ❑ Adoption papers   _____
- ❑ Annulment decrees   _____
- ❑ Athletic awards   _____
- ❑ Birth certificates   _____
- ❑ Change-of-name certificates   _____
- ❑ Civic awards   _____
- ❑ Death certificates   _____
- ❑ Divorce decrees or judgments   _____
- ❑ Dramatic awards   _____
- ❑ Educational awards   _____
- ❑ Educational transcripts   _____
- ❑ Marriage certificates   _____
- ❑ Military awards   _____
- ❑ Military separation papers   _____
- ❑ Naturalization papers   _____
- ❑ Newspaper articles   _____
- ❑ Organization awards   _____
- ❑ Organization membership certificates _____
- ❑ _____   _____
- ❑ _____   _____

Insurance

Safe-Deposit Box   **Other Locations**

- ❑ Life insurance policies   _____
- ❑ Medical and health insurance policies _____
- ❑ Residence insurance policies   _____
- ❑ Vehicle insurance policies   _____
- ❑ _____   _____
- ❑ _____   _____
- ❑ _____   _____

Other Benefits

Safe-Deposit Box

❑ 401(k) agreements
❑ IRA agreements
❑ Keogh plan agreements
❑ Medicare card
❑ Military separation papers
❑ Pension agreements
❑ Railroad retirement documents
❑ Social Security card
❑ Workers' compensation award
❑ _____
❑ _____

Other Locations

_____
_____
_____
_____
_____
_____
_____
_____
_____
_____
_____

Banking and Savings

Safe-Deposit Box

❑ Cash
❑ Checking account statements
❑ Credit union account statements
❑ Savings account books or statements
❑ _____
❑ _____

Other Locations

_____
_____
_____
_____
_____
_____

Will, Trust, Agreements, etc.

Safe-Deposit Box

❑ Living will
❑ Powers of attorney
❑ Durable power of attorney
❑ Health care proxy (durable power
   of attorney for health care)
❑ Trust agreement
❑ Trust agreement
❑ Trust agreement
❑ Will and codicils
❑ _____

Other Locations

_____
_____
_____

_____
_____
_____
_____
_____
_____

Securities, Real Estate, and Miscellaneous Assets

Safe-Deposit Box

Other Locations

- ❑ Business records _____
- ❑ Decrees _____
- ❑ Deeds _____
- ❑ Home improvement records _____
- ❑ Judgments _____
- ❑ Leases _____
- ❑ Mortgages _____
- ❑ Patents or copyrights _____
- ❑ Rental property records _____
- ❑ Investment statements _____
- ❑ Vehicle certificates of title _____
- ❑ _____ _____
- ❑ _____ _____

Final Wishes

Safe-Deposit Box

Other Locations

- ❑ Body bequeathal papers _____
- ❑ Cemetery deed _____
- ❑ Funeral prearrangement agreement _____
- ❑ Mausoleum deed _____
- ❑ Uniform donor card _____
- ❑ _____ _____

Miscellaneous Information

Safe-Deposit Box

Other Locations

- ❑ Animal care information _____
- ❑ Burglar alarm information _____
- ❑ Child care information _____
- ❑ Letters to be sent upon my death _____
- ❑ List of hiding places for valuables _____
- ❑ Property care information _____
- ❑ Tax records _____
- ❑ _____ _____

Keys and Combinations

Safe-Deposit Box

- ❑ Keys to homes
- ❑ Keys to other real estate
- ❑ Keys to post office boxes
- ❑ Keys to safe-deposit box(es)
- ❑ Keys to vehicles
- ❑ Other keys
- ❑ Combination to lock #1
- ❑ Combination to lock #2
- ❑ Combination to lock #3

Other Locations

_____

_____

_____

_____

_____

_____

_____

_____

_____

Other

Safe-Deposit Box

- ❑ Cassettes
- ❑ Computer and other electronic media
- ❑ Photos
- ❑ Videos
- ❑ _____
- ❑ _____
- ❑ _____

Other Locations

_____

_____

_____

_____

_____

_____

_____

Products and Services with Passwords

Remember to provide and update passwords for any products or services that are secured.

Such items might include:

- Home safe
- Personal computers
- Gates
- E-mail accounts
- Lockers
- Home alarm system
- Drawers and cabinets

- Online services
- Cell phones
- Web hosting services
- Personal digital assistant (PDA)
- Internet service provider
- Pager
- Children's day care or school access codes

Product/service _____

User name _____

Password/PIN or key location _____

Product/service _____

User name _____

Password/PIN or key location _____

Product/service _____

User name _____

Password/PIN or key location _____

Product/Service _____

User name _____

Password/PIN or key location _____

Product/service _____

User name _____

Password/PIN or key location _____

Product/service _____

User name _____

Password/PIN or key location _____

Product/service _____

User name _____

Password/PIN or key location _____

Products and Services with Passwords (continued)

Product/service _____

User name _____

Password/PIN or key location _____

Product/service _____

User name _____

Password/PIN or key location _____

Product/service _____

User name _____

Password/PIN or key location _____

Product/service _____

User name _____

Password/PIN or key location _____

Product/service _____

User name _____

Password/PIN or key location _____

Product/service _____

User name _____

Password/PIN or key location _____

Product/service _____

User name _____

Password/PIN or key location _____

Product/service _____

User name _____

Password/PIN or key location _____

Product/service _____

User name _____

Password/PIN or key location _____

Product/service _____

User name _____

Password/PIN or key location _____

Lifefolio

Personal History

Residences

Places I Have Lived

Dates _____ Address _____
City_____ State _____

Dates _____ Address _____
City_____ State _____

Dates _____ Address _____
City_____ State _____

Dates _____ Address _____
City_____ State _____

Dates _____ Address _____
City_____ State _____

Dates _____ Address _____
City_____ State _____

Dates _____ Address _____
City_____ State _____

Dates _____ Address _____
City_____ State _____

Dates _____ Address _____
City_____ State _____

Dates _____ Address _____
City_____ State _____

Dates _____ Address _____
City_____ State _____

Dates _____ Address _____
City_____ State _____

Dates _____ Address _____
City_____ State _____

Educational Background

Elementary Schools I Attended

Name of school_____

Grades attended _____ Dates attended _____

Address _____

City_____ State _____

Name of school_____

Grades attended _____ Dates attended _____

Address _____

City_____ State _____

Name of school_____

Grades attended _____ Dates attended _____

Address _____

City_____ State _____

Comments _____

Junior High Schools or Middle Schools I Attended

Name of school_____

Grades attended _____ Dates attended _____

Address _____

City_____ State _____

Name of school_____

Grades attended _____ Dates attended _____

Address _____

City_____ State _____

Name of school_____

Grades attended _____ Dates attended _____

Address _____

City_____ State _____

Comments _____

High Schools or Preparatory Schools I Attended

Name of school_____

Grades attended _____ Dates attended _____

Address _____

City_____ State _____

Name of school_____

Grades attended _____ Dates attended _____

Address _____

City_____ State _____

Comments _____

_____

_____

Institutions of Higher Learning I Attended

Name of school_____

Dates attended _____ Degree earned _____

Course of study _____

Address _____

City_____ State _____

Name of school_____

Dates attended _____ Degree earned _____

Course of study _____

Address _____

City_____ State _____

Name of school_____

Dates attended _____ Degree earned _____

Course of study _____

Address _____

City_____ State _____

Comments _____

_____

_____

_____

Military Records

Did you serve in United States Military?   ❑ Yes   ❑ No
If yes, fill in the information below.

Branch of service _____ Grade or rank _____
Active service dates _____ Place _____

Branch of service _____ Grade or rank _____
Active service dates _____ Place _____

Branch of service _____ Grade or rank _____
Active service dates _____ Place _____

Branch of service _____ Grade or rank _____
Active service dates _____ Place _____

Branch of service _____ Grade or rank _____
Active service dates _____ Place _____

Branch of service _____ Grade or rank _____
Active service dates _____ Place _____

Branch of service _____ Grade or rank _____
Active service dates _____ Place _____

List any military decorations here. _____
_____
_____
_____
_____

Provide a résumé of your military career here. _____
_____
_____
_____
_____
_____
_____

Work Background

Here are the names of my primary employers (most current first).

Employer _____

Dates _____ Type of work_____

Address _____

City_____ State _____ Phone _____

Employer _____

Dates _____ Type of work_____

Address _____

City_____ State _____ Phone _____

Employer _____

Dates _____ Type of work_____

Address _____

City_____ State _____ Phone _____

Employer _____

Dates _____ Type of work_____

Address _____

City_____ State _____ Phone _____

Employer _____

Dates _____ Type of work_____

Address _____

City_____ State _____ Phone _____

Employer _____

Dates _____ Type of work_____

Address _____

City_____ State _____ Phone _____

Employer _____

Dates _____ Type of work_____

Address _____

City_____ State _____ Phone _____

Work Background (continued)

- ❏ I retired from work on (date) _____.
- ❏ I am presently employed (fill in details below).

Employer _____

Dates _____ Type of work_____

Address _____

City_____ State _____ Phone _____

Comments _____

_____

_____

_____

_____

_____

_____

_____

_____

_____

_____

_____

Describe any interesting facts and experiences over the years concerning employment.

_____

_____

_____

_____

_____

_____

_____

_____

_____

_____

_____

_____

_____

Business Interests

Do you have any active business interests? ❏ Yes ❏ No

If yes, briefly describe and indicate location of documentation and contact information for business partners._____

_____

_____

_____

_____

_____

_____

_____

_____

_____

_____

_____

_____

_____

_____

_____

_____

_____

_____

_____

_____

_____

_____

_____

_____

_____

_____

_____

Health Care Medical History

Are there any issues in your medical history that should be documented for future generations? ❑ Yes ❑ No

If yes, fill in the information below.

Health care issue _____

Date of onset _____

Surgery/treatment received_____

Location of related documents_____

Health care issue _____

Date of onset _____

Surgery/treatment received_____

Location of related documents_____

Health care issue _____

Date of onset _____

Surgery/treatment received_____

Location of related documents_____

Health care issue _____

Date of onset _____

Surgery/treatment received_____

Location of related documents_____

Health care issue _____

Date of onset _____

Surgery/treatment received_____

Location of related documents_____

Health care issue _____

Date of onset _____

Surgery/treatment received_____

Location of related documents_____

Health care issue _____

Date of onset _____

Surgery/treatment received_____

Location of related documents_____

Health Care Medical History (continued)

Health care issue _____

Date of onset _____

Surgery/treatment received_____

Location of related documents_____

Health care issue _____

Date of onset _____

Surgery/treatment received_____

Location of related documents_____

Health care issue _____

Date of onset _____

Surgery/treatment received_____

Location of related documents_____

Health care issue _____

Date of onset _____

Surgery/treatment received_____

Location of related documents_____

Health care issue _____

Date of onset _____

Surgery/treatment received_____

Location of related documents_____

Health care issue _____

Date of onset _____

Surgery/treatment received_____

Location of related documents_____

Health care issue _____

Date of onset _____

Surgery/treatment received_____

Location of related documents_____

Health care issue _____

Date of onset _____

Surgery/treatment received_____

Location of related documents_____

Lifefolio

Financial Assets, Liabilities, and Insurance

Assets

Bank Accounts

Bank/credit union _____

Bank address _____

City _____ State _____ Phone _____

Account type _____ Account number _____

User name _____ Password _____

Bank/credit union _____

Bank address _____

City _____ State _____ Phone _____

Account type _____ Account number _____

User name _____ Password _____

Bank/credit union _____

Bank address _____

City _____ State _____ Phone _____

Account type _____ Account number _____

User name _____ Password _____

Bank/credit union _____

Bank address _____

City _____ State _____ Phone _____

Account type _____ Account number _____

User name _____ Password _____

Bank/credit union _____

Bank address _____

City _____ State _____ Phone _____

Account type _____ Account number _____

User name _____ Password _____

Bank/credit union _____

Bank address _____

City _____ State _____ Phone _____

Account type _____ Account number _____

User name _____ Password _____

Investment Accounts (Stocks, Bonds, Mutual Funds, 401(k) Accounts)

Account name _____

Account number _____ Current value _____

Company address _____

City_____ State _____ Phone _____

Beneficiary name _____

Tax status (taxable/tax-deferred/tax-exempt) _____

Account name _____

Account number _____ Current value _____

Company address _____

City_____ State _____ Phone _____

Beneficiary name _____

Tax status (taxable/tax-deferred/tax-exempt) _____

Account name _____

Account number _____ Current value _____

Company address _____

City_____ State _____ Phone _____

Beneficiary name _____

Tax status (taxable/tax-deferred/tax-exempt) _____

Account name _____

Account number _____ Current value _____

Company address _____

City_____ State _____ Phone _____

Beneficiary name _____

Tax status (taxable/tax-deferred/tax-exempt) _____

Account name _____

Account number _____ Current value _____

Company address _____

City_____ State _____ Phone _____

Beneficiary name _____

Tax status (taxable/tax-deferred/tax-exempt) _____

Pension Plans

Are you a member of a pension plan?   ❑ Yes   ❑ No

If yes, do you currently receive benefits?   ❑ Yes   ❑ No

Plan name _____

Company address _____

City_____ State _____ Phone _____

Beneficiary name _____

Location of documentation_____

Are you a member of a second pension plan?   ❑ Yes   ❑ No

If yes, do you currently receive benefits?   ❑ Yes   ❑ No

Plan name _____

Company address _____

City_____ State _____ Phone _____

Beneficiary name _____

Location of documentation_____

Are you a member of a third pension plan?   ❑ Yes   ❑ No

If yes, do you currently receive benefits?   ❑ Yes   ❑ No

Plan name _____

Company address _____

City_____ State _____ Phone _____

Beneficiary name _____

Location of documentation_____

Social Security

Do you currently receive a Social Security benefit?   ❑ Yes   ❑ No

Monthly amount $_____   ❑ Check   ❑ Direct deposit

Bank/credit union _____

Bank address_____

City_____ State _____ Phone _____

Account number _____

Veterans' Benefits

Do you receive a retirement benefit from the U.S. government. ❑ Yes ❑ No

Amount $_____ ❑ Check ❑ Direct deposit

Bank/credit union _____

Bank address_____

City_____ State _____ Phone _____

Account number _____

Beneficiary name _____

Location of documentation_____

Liabilities (Financial Commitments)

Rent or Mortgage Payments

Property _____

Amount _____ Due date _____

Lender address _____

City_____ State _____ Phone _____

Property _____

Amount _____ Due date _____

Lender address _____

City_____ State _____ Phone _____

Property _____

Amount _____ Due date _____

Lender address _____

City_____ State _____ Phone _____

Property _____

Amount _____ Due date _____

Lender address _____

City_____ State _____ Phone _____

Outstanding Loans

Purpose _____

Amount _____ Due date _____

Lender address _____

City_____ State _____ Phone _____

Purpose _____

Amount _____ Due date _____

Lender address _____

City_____ State _____ Phone _____

Purpose _____

Amount _____ Due date _____

Lender address _____

City_____ State _____ Phone _____

Bills Paid by Automatic Payment Plan

Company _____
Account number _____ Due date _____
Address _____
City_____ State _____ Phone _____
Day account is debited _____
User name _____ Password _____

Company _____
Account number _____ Due date _____
Address _____
City_____ State _____ Phone _____
Day account is debited _____
User name _____ Password _____

Company _____
Account number _____ Due date _____
Address _____
City_____ State _____ Phone _____
Day account is debited _____
User name _____ Password _____

Company _____
Account number _____ Due date _____
Address _____
City_____ State _____ Phone _____
Day account is debited _____
User name _____ Password _____

Company _____
Account number _____ Due date _____
Address _____
City_____ State _____ Phone _____
Day account is debited _____
User name _____ Password _____

Credit/Debit Cards

Company _____

Account number _____ Due date _____

Address _____

City_____ State _____ Phone _____

Approximate balance due _____

Company _____

Account number _____ Due date _____

Address _____

City_____ State _____ Phone _____

Approximate balance due _____

Company _____

Account number _____ Due date _____

Address _____

City_____ State _____ Phone _____

Approximate balance due _____

Company _____

Account number _____ Due date _____

Address _____

City_____ State _____ Phone _____

Approximate balance due _____

Company _____

Account number _____ Due date _____

Address _____

City_____ State _____ Phone _____

Approximate balance due _____

Company _____

Account number _____ Due date _____

Address _____

City_____ State _____ Phone _____

Approximate balance due _____

Debtors and Creditors

Do you have a recent credit report? ❑ Yes ❑ No

If yes, where is a copy of the report located? _____

Does anyone owe you money? ❑ Yes ❑ No

If yes, fill in the information below.

Name _____

Address _____

City_____ State _____ Phone _____

Amount _____ Date of loan _____

Terms _____

Name _____

Address _____

City_____ State _____ Phone _____

Amount _____ Date of Loan _____

Terms _____

Do you owe anyone money? ❑ Yes ❑ No

If yes, fill in information below.

Name _____

Address _____

City_____ State _____ Phone _____

Amount _____ Date of loan _____

Terms _____

Name _____

Address _____

City_____ State _____ Phone _____

Amount _____ Date of loan _____

Terms _____

Where are the loan agreements or promissory notes located? _____

_____

_____

Insurance

Life Insurance

Company _____

Company address _____

City_____ State _____ Phone _____

Policy number _____ Death benefit_____

Person covered _____

Beneficiary name _____

Location of policy_____

Company _____

Company address _____

City_____ State _____ Phone _____

Policy number _____ Death benefit_____

Person covered _____

Beneficiary name _____

Location of policy_____

Company _____

Company address _____

City_____ State _____ Phone _____

Policy number _____ Death benefit_____

Person covered _____

Beneficiary name _____

Location of policy_____

Company _____

Company address _____

City_____ State _____ Phone _____

Policy number _____ Death benefit_____

Person covered _____

Beneficiary name _____

Location of policy_____

Health Insurance/Hospitalization

Company _____

Company address _____

City_____ State _____ Phone _____

Policy number_____

Person covered _____

Location of policy _____

Company _____

Company address _____

City_____ State _____ Phone _____

Policy number_____

Person covered _____

Location of policy _____

Company _____

Company address _____

City_____ State _____ Phone _____

Policy number_____

Person covered _____

Location of policy _____

Company _____

Company address _____

City_____ State _____ Phone _____

Policy number_____

Person covered _____

Location of policy _____

Company _____

Company address _____

City_____ State _____ Phone _____

Policy number_____

Person covered _____

Location of policy _____

Long-Term Care Insurance

Company _____

Company address _____

City_____ State _____ Phone _____

Policy number _____ Death benefit_____

Person covered _____

Benefit amount per day _____ Benefit period _____ Waiting period _____

Location of policy_____

Company _____

Company address _____

City_____ State _____ Phone _____

Policy number _____ Death benefit_____

Person covered _____

Benefit amount per day _____ Benefit period _____ Waiting period _____

Location of policy_____

Company _____

Company address _____

City_____ State _____ Phone _____

Policy number _____ Death benefit_____

Person covered _____

Benefit amount per day _____ Benefit period _____ Waiting period _____

Location of policy_____

Company _____

Company address _____

City_____ State _____ Phone _____

Policy number _____ Death benefit_____

Person covered _____

Benefit amount per day _____ Benefit period _____ Waiting period _____

Location of policy_____

Memberships

Include any memberships to organizations that should be cancelled or transferred. Also be sure to include airline frequent flyer programs and other affinity programs where benefits might be transferred.

Organization_____

Organization address _____

City_____ State _____ Phone _____

Member name _____

Member number _____

Membership card location _____

Transfer to whom or cancel? _____

Organization_____

Organization address _____

City_____ State _____ Phone _____

Member name _____

Member number _____

Membership card location _____

Transfer to whom or cancel? _____

Organization_____

Organization address _____

City_____ State _____ Phone _____

Member name _____

Member number _____

Membership card location _____

Transfer to whom or cancel? _____

Organization_____

Organization address _____

City_____ State _____ Phone _____

Member name _____

Member number _____

Membership card location _____

Transfer to whom or cancel? _____

Memberships (continued)

Organization_____

Organization address _____

City_____ State _____ Phone _____

Member name _____

Member number _____

Membership card location _____

Transfer to whom or cancel? _____

Organization_____

Organization address _____

City_____ State _____ Phone _____

Member name _____

Member number _____

Membership card location _____

Transfer to whom or cancel? _____

Organization_____

Organization address _____

City_____ State _____ Phone _____

Member name _____

Member number _____

Membership card location _____

Transfer to whom or cancel? _____

Organization_____

Organization address _____

City_____ State _____ Phone _____

Member name _____

Member number _____

Membership card location _____

Transfer to whom or cancel? _____

Organization_____

Organization address _____

City_____ State _____ Phone _____

Member name _____

Member number _____

Membership card location _____

Transfer to whom or cancel? _____

Lifefolio

Instructions and Wishes to Be Fulfilled

Documentation

Living Will

Do you have a living will?   ❑ Yes   ❑ No

If yes, where is your living will kept?_____

If no, do you plan on creating one?   ❑ Yes   ❑ No

Health Care Proxy

Do you have a declaration prepared that details the type of   ❑ Yes   ❑ No
care you want (or don't want) if you become incapacitated?

Where is your health care declaration kept? _____

Do you have a durable power of attorney health care proxy?   ❑ Yes   ❑ No

Who is named as your health care proxy? _____

Where is your healthy care proxy document kept? _____

Directives for Life-Support Measures

Have you discussed your wishes regarding life-support measures   ❑ Yes   ❑ No
with your doctor, spouse, or other trusted individuals?

If yes, with whom and when? _____

Organ Donation

Do you want to donate your organs or body for transplant,   ❑ Yes   ❑ No
medical research, or education?

If yes, have you explained these wishes in your will?   ❑ Yes   ❑ No

Do you have an organ-donor card?   ❑ Yes   ❑ No

Does your driver's license indicate that you are an organ donor?   ❑ Yes   ❑ No

Briefly describe what you want donated and for what purpose. Be sure to share these wishes with trusted family members so that there is no confusion about your wishes.

_____

_____

_____

_____

_____

_____

_____

Living Arrangements

How and where do you want to live as you grow older?

- Location close to family, friends, or within a specific community
- Retirement community considerations
- Assisted-living considerations
- Assistance with current residence

Use this space to document your wishes.

_____

_____

_____

_____

_____

_____

_____

_____

_____

_____

_____

_____

_____

_____

_____

_____

_____

_____

_____

_____

_____

_____

_____

_____

_____

Final Wishes and Directives

What are your final wishes and directives to be followed at the time of your passing?

- Instructions for your family or named responsible individual
- Instructions for the executor of your will and trustee of your trust
- Specific bequests of items
- Wishes for your funeral and burial

Use this space to document your wishes.

_____

_____

_____

_____

_____

_____

_____

_____

_____

_____

_____

_____

_____

_____

_____

_____

_____

_____

_____

_____

_____

_____

_____

_____

_____

_____

_____

_____

Will

Do you have a will?   ❑ Yes   ❑ No
Where is the original located? _____

Is there another copy?   ❑ Yes   ❑ No
If so, where is it?_____

When was the will last dated/updated? _____

Durable Power of Attorney

Do you have a durable power of attorney?   ❑ Yes   ❑ No
If yes, fill in the information below.
Name _____
Address _____
City_____ State _____ Phone _____
Where is the original located? _____

Is there another copy?   ❑ Yes   ❑ No
If so, where is it?_____

Do you have a family attorney?   ❑ Yes   ❑ No
If yes, fill in the information below.
Name _____
Address _____
City_____ State _____ Phone _____

Trust Funds

Have you created any trusts?   ❑ Yes   ❑ No
If yes, what is the purpose of the trust? _____
Is the trust agreement part of your will?   ❑ Yes   ❑ No
Where are the trust papers located? _____
Who manages this for you?
Name _____
Address _____
City_____ State _____ Phone _____

Funeral Arrangements

Have you made funeral arrangements on your behalf?   ❏ Yes   ❏ No

If yes, fill in the information below.

Funeral home _____

Address _____

City_____ State _____ Phone _____

If arrangements have been made, where is the documentation located? _____

_____

Have you set out instructions for burial/cremation?   ❏ Yes   ❏ No

Are these instructions in your will?   ❏ Yes   ❏ No

If yes, where are they located? _____

Do you own a cemetery lot?   ❏ Yes   ❏ No

If yes, fill in the information below.

Location _____

Address _____

City_____ State _____ Phone _____

Have you provided for its ongoing care?   ❏ Yes   ❏ No

Where is the cemetery deed kept?_____

Lifefolio

Legacy

Values and Life Lessons

Ethics and Moral Teachings

What virtues and values would you like to see continued throughout your family's generations?

- Important values that guide your family
- Principles on the treatment of environment, country, and property
- Virtues that bring out the best in you and your children
- Contributions to specific charities or nonprofit organizations

Use this space to document your wishes.

_____
_____
_____
_____
_____
_____
_____
_____
_____
_____

Have you named any charities or other organizations as beneficiaries in your will?   ❑ Yes   ❑ No

If yes, fill in the information below.

Organization _____
Address _____
City_____ State _____ Phone _____

Organization _____
Address _____
City_____ State _____ Phone _____

Organization _____
Address _____
City_____ State _____ Phone _____

Organization _____
Address _____
City_____ State _____ Phone _____

Faith and Religion

What religious traditions would you like to see continued throughout the generations?

- Belief doctrines within your family
- Cultural religious traditions and the values they represent
- Religious items to be passed down to future generations
- Contributions to specific religious organizations

Use this space to document your wishes.

_____
_____
_____
_____
_____
_____
_____
_____
_____
_____
_____

Have you named any religious organizations as beneficiaries in your will?   ❑ Yes   ❑ No

If yes, fill in the information below.

Organization _____
Address _____
City_____ State _____ Phone _____

Organization _____
Address _____
City_____ State _____ Phone _____

Organization _____
Address _____
City_____ State _____ Phone _____

Organization _____
Address _____
City_____ State _____ Phone _____

Family Traditions and Stories

What family rituals would you like to see continue throughout the generations?

- History from past generation that provides guidance
- Holiday traditions, celebrations, and special life events
- Family trips, reunions, and gatherings with friends
- Favorite stories either documented or shared

Use this space to document your wishes.

_____

_____

_____

_____

_____

_____

_____

_____

_____

_____

_____

_____

_____

_____

_____

_____

_____

_____

_____

_____

_____

_____

_____

_____

_____

_____

_____

_____

Personal Possessions of Emotional Value

Do you have belongings of emotional value?

- Collections with emotional value that may not have significant financial value
- Memorabilia with emotional value that may not have significant financial value
- Specific items that are associated with fond memories, sentiments, or remembrance
- Designated plan on how items are distributed

Use this space to document your wishes. Be sure to include information regarding where these collections are located and any special directions for the ongoing care of them.

_____
_____
_____
_____
_____
_____
_____
_____
_____
_____
_____
_____
_____
_____
_____
_____
_____
_____
_____
_____
_____
_____
_____
_____
_____

Pictures, Journals, and Family History

Are there items that document your life and/or family's life that you would like to see passed on to future generations?

- Photo albums, electronic photos, videos, and home movies
- Journals, diaries, travel journals, and scrapbooks
- Family trees and genealogical studies
- Passports and other important documents

Use this space to document your wishes. Be sure to indicate where these items are located and who has access to them.

_____

_____

_____

_____

_____

_____

_____

_____

_____

_____

_____

_____

_____

_____

_____

_____

_____

_____

_____

_____

_____

_____

_____

_____

_____

Financial Gifts

Do you plan on making any specific financial gifts to anyone in your will?   ❏ Yes   ❏ No
If yes, fill in the information below.

Name _____
Address _____
City_____ State _____ Phone _____
Amount _____
Terms _____

Name _____
Address _____
City_____ State _____ Phone _____
Amount _____
Terms _____

Name _____
Address _____
City_____ State _____ Phone _____
Amount _____
Terms _____

Name _____
Address _____
City_____ State _____ Phone _____
Amount _____
Terms _____

Name _____
Address _____
City_____ State _____ Phone _____
Amount _____
Terms _____

Name _____
Address _____
City_____ State _____ Phone _____
Amount _____
Terms _____

Household Items

Are there items in your household that hold significant emotional value though they may not have much financial value?

- Children's toys, books, or mementos
- Articles of clothing that evoke fond memories
- Artwork such as quilts, paintings, crafts, or carvings
- Household items such as cookware, furniture, tools, books, or computer equipment.

Use this space to document your wishes. Be sure to indicate where these items are located and who has access to them..

_____

_____

_____

_____

_____

_____

_____

_____

_____

_____

_____

_____

_____

_____

_____

_____

_____

_____

_____

_____

_____

_____

_____

_____

_____

_____

Book Bob Mauterstock for Your Meeting or Conference

Bob Mauterstock is recognized as an expert in the areas of retirement income planning, long-term care planning, and veterans' benefits. He has been a financial advisor to hundreds of families over the last 30 years and has helped them achieve a worry-free, comfortable retirement. In addition, he has helped many families deal with the chronic illness of a family member. He has worked with them to create a long-term care plan using Medicare, Medicaid, Veterans' Benefits, and other resources to protect their assets.

He is an accomplished speaker and authority on the financial concerns of the elderly. He has developed a program entitled "Leaving Your Mark" to inspire elderly parents to work together with their adult children to preserve their legacy.

After graduating from Princeton University in 1968, Bob served as a Navy Helicopter Pilot with Helicopter Combat Support Squadron Four from 1968-1974. He received a Master's Degree in Education from the University of Connecticut and holds the designations of Certified Financial Planner (CFP) and Chartered Financial Consultant (ChFC). Bob is also Certified in Long-Term Care (CLTC).

Bob lives with his lovely wife, Mary, on a quiet pond in Brewster, Massachusetts. He spends his free time flying his model airplanes on the beautiful beaches of Cape Cod near his home. Their daughter, Stephanie, lives in New York City where she runs a s charter school created to offer a quality educational alternative to inner-city kids.

Learn more about Bob and his services at his websites www.parentcareplanning.com and www.veteransmass.com.

Order More Copies of This Book

Online	Place your order online at www.parentcareplanning.com
Phone	Call 508-246-7564 Monday through Friday 8 a.m. to 5 p.m. EST
Postal Mail	Send your completed order form to Bob Mauterstock P.O. Box 570 Brewster, MA 02631 USA

Can We Talk? A Financial Guide for Baby Boomers   Paperback, 130 pages
Assisting Their Elderly Parents   _____ x $20.00 = _____

Please add 5% sales tax for orders shipped to Massachusetts addresses.

Shipping and Handling

USA: Add $4 for the first book and $1 for each additional book.
International: $9 for the first book; $5 for each additional book.

Payment

❏ Check or Money Order Enclosed

To purchase your book using a credit card, go to www.parentcareplanning.com.

Your Information

Name _____

Address _____

City_____ State _____ Zip _____

Telephone _____

E-mail address _____

CPSIA information can be obtained at www.ICGtesting.com
Printed in the USA
BVOW06s0200220514

354169BV00002B/6/P